# COME AND BE HEALED

By Todd Levin

First Printing 1994
Reprinted 2002
Revised 2013

Todd Levin Ministries International
P.O. Box 826
Belle Vernon, PA 15012
www.toddlevinministries.com



Printed in the United States of America
Cover Photo by Danny Levin

Come And Be Healed
ISBN-13: 978-1484032800
ISBN-10: 1484032802

# COME AND BE HEALED

## CONTENTS

# A PRACTICAL COMPREHENSIVE STUDY GUIDE

# INTRODUCTION

Jesus said in John's Gospel chapter 10:10, *"the thief comes only to steal, to kill, and to destroy, I am come that you might have life and have it more abundantly."* Does this include healing for the body as well as for the soul? Satan has sold the church a bill of lies in believing that sickness is just "part of life." Others believe that sickness is sent from above to perfect God's will in us. No thing could be further from the truth as revealed to us from God's Word.

When Christians wake up to the fact and realize that Jesus came to give abundant life, they will see that sickness and disease is not the plan or will of God for His children but rather indirectly the consequence of man's sin in the garden.

In this study we will be answering a series of questions from a Biblical viewpoint such as:

(1) Why did Jesus come?
(2) What are the origin and cause of sickness and disease?
(3) How did sickness and disease enter into the world?
(4) Does God have favorites or is healing for everyone?
(5) Are the days of miracles over or is God still the same?
(6) Did Jesus redeem us from our diseases when He atoned for our sins?
(7) Is God glorified in our sickness and disease?
(8) Does a Christian have to suffer?
(9) Who brings tests and trials?
(10) Does God permit persecution?

These and many other questions we will be answering in our study of *Come and be Healed.* Please read this guide very carefully with an open heart allowing the Holy Spirit to speak to you through the scriptures. May God bless your study of His Word!

Sincerely yours,

Todd Levin

# LESSON 1

# THE ORIGIN OF SICKNESS AND DISEASE

## I. WHERE DID IT ALL BEGIN?

1. Oppression comes directly from satan, not from God. They're not working together. God wants His children to enjoy life to its fullest whereas satan is out to destroy life by indirectly striking at God each time he comes against the object of God's love which is you!

> *"The thief comes only in order to steal and kill and destroy. I came that they may have and enjoy life, and have it in abundance (to the full, till it overflows."*
>
> **John 10:10 (AMP)**
>
> *"How God anointed Jesus of Nazareth with the Holy Ghost and with power: who went about doing good, and healing all that were oppressed of the devil; for God was with him."*
>
> **Acts 10:38**
>
> *"For the Son of man is not come to destroy men's lives, but to save them."*
> **Luke 9:56**

2. Satan is the one who binds you, but God is the one who looses and sets you free.

> *"Then was brought unto him one possessed with a devil, blind, and dumb: and he healed him, insomuch that the blind and dumb both spake and saw."*
> **Matthew 12:22**
>
> *"And, behold, there was a woman which had a spirit of infirmity eighteen years, and was bowed together, and could in no wise lift up herself. And when Jesus saw her, he called her to him, and said unto her, Woman, thou art loosed from thine infirmity. And he laid his hands on her: and immediately she was*

*made straight, and glorified God. And the ruler of the synagogue answered with indignation, because that Jesus had healed on the sabbath day, and said unto the people, There are six days in which men ought to work: in them therefore come and be healed, and not on the sabbath day. The Lord then answered him, and said, Thou hypocrite, doth not each one of you on the sabbath loose his ox or his ass from the stall, and lead him away to watering? And ought not this woman, being a daughter of Abraham, whom Satan hath bound, lo, these eighteen years, be loosed from this bond on the sabbath day? And when he had said these things, all his adversaries were ashamed: and all the people rejoiced for all the glorious things that were done by him."*

**Luke 13:10-17**

*"And one of the multitude answered and said, Master, I have brought unto thee my son, which hath a dumb spirit; And wheresoever he taketh him, he teareth him: and he foameth, and gnasheth with his teeth, and pineth away: and I spake to thy disciples that they should cast him out; and they could not. He answereth him, and saith, O faithless generation, how long shall I be with you? How long shall I suffer you? Bring him unto me. And they brought him unto him: and when he saw him, straightway the spirit tare him; and he fell on the ground, and wallowed foaming. And he asked his father, How long is it ago since this came unto him? And he said, Of a child. And ofttimes it hath cast him into the fire, and into the waters, to destroy him: but if thou canst do any thing, have compassion on us, and help us. Jesus said unto him, If thou canst believe, all things are possible to him that believeth. And straightway the father of the child cried out, and said with tears, Lord, I believe; help thou mine unbelief. When Jesus saw that the people came running together, he rebuked the foul spirit, saying unto him, Thou dumb and deaf spirit, I charge thee, come out of him, and enter no more into him. And the spirit cried, and rent him sore, and came out of him: and he was as one dead; insomuch that many said, He is dead. But Jesus took him by the hand, and lifted him up; and he arose."*

**Mark 9:17-27**

3. Satan and demons are the agents that bring sickness and disease to people. The bible shows that sickness comes directly from satan.

*"So went Satan forth from the presence of the LORD, and smote Job with sore boils from the sole of his foot unto his crown."*

**Job 2:7**

A. It is scripturally true that satan **cannot** put sickness or disease on our bodies unless we give him the privilege due to the fact that Jesus has purchased us for himself with His own blood. Below are several scriptures that show we are indeed children of God, redeemed by the blood of the Lamb!

> *"In whom we have redemption through his blood, the forgiveness of sins, according to the riches of his grace...But now in Christ Jesus ye who sometimes were far off are made nigh by the blood of Christ...Now therefore ye are no more strangers and foreigners, but fellow citizens with the saints, and of the household of God."*
>
> **Ephesians 1:7; 2:13,19**
>
> *"In whom we have redemption through his blood, even the forgiveness of sins."*
>
> **Colossians 1:14**
>
> *"Neither by the blood of goats and calves, but by his own blood he entered in once into the holy place, having obtained eternal redemption for us."*
>
> **Hebrews 9:12**
>
> *"Wherefore Jesus also, that he might sanctify the people with his own blood, suffered without the gate."*
>
> **Hebrews 13:12**
>
> *"Forasmuch as ye know that ye were not redeemed with corruptible things, as silver and gold, from your vain conversation received by tradition from your fathers; But with the precious blood of Christ, as of a lamb without blemish and without spot."*
>
> **1 Peter 1:18,19**
>
> *"And from Jesus Christ, who is the faithful witness, and the first begotten of the dead, and the prince of the kings of the earth. Unto him that loved us, and washed us from our sins in his own blood."*
>
> **Revelation 1:5**

B. Now as a child of God, we are no longer part of satan's family. Therefore he cannot exercise authority over us because we are not of his household, but God's.

> *"Who hath delivered us from the power of darkness, and hath translated us into the kingdom of his dear Son."*
>
> **Colossians 1:13**

> *"For he has rescued us from the dominion of darkness and brought us into the kingdom of the Son he loves."*
>
> **Colossians 1:13 (NIV)**

C. If you are living in open sin, your faith will not work for you. Sin throws the door open for satan to oppress you. Sin gives satan the legal right to come right on in. Therefore, keep the door closed! When the apostle Paul wrote to the believers in Ephesus, he was very specific in regards to messing around with the enemy.

> *"Afterward Jesus findeth him in the temple, and said unto him, Behold, thou art made whole: sin no more, lest a worse thing come unto thee."*
>
> **John 5:15**
>
> *"Neither give place to the devil."*
>
> **Ephesians 4:27**

D. What many Christians call faith is actually foolishness.

- Foolishness will also throw open the door for the enemy to come in and to oppress you.
- What many call faith is no more than foolishness and presumption.

> **EX**: Going outside in freezing weather without a coat.
> **EX**: Sleeping with a window open above your head while cold air is blowing in on you all night.

E. How come when I'm living right, thinking right, and talking right that I'm still attacked? I thought I was exempt from enemy attacks once I became a Christian.

**Answer** - What satan is trying to do is to get you to open the door. When he attacks you, that's the same thing as somebody knocking on your door. Don't answer it. If you're foolish enough to open the door, then he's coming in.

- Along with the darts of pain, symptoms and sickness that the enemy sends to your body, immediately he'll also sow the thought in your mind, "*You're going to be sick. Maybe that is a tumour. You're going to die, etc.*"
- As soon as you accept that thought as yours and start believing it, confessing it and acting on that thought, then it opens the door to give satan a legal right to oppress your body.
- Notice what Jesus said, that the way we accept a thought is by saying.

> *"Therefore take no thought, saying, What shall we eat? Or, what shall we drink? Or, Wherewithal shall we be clothed?"*
>
> **Matthew 6:31**

**What should you do instead?**

> *"Casting down imaginations, and every high thing that exalteth itself against the knowledge of God, and bringing into captivity every thought to the obedience of Christ."*
>
> **2 Corinthians 10:5**
>
> *"Submit yourselves therefore to God. Resist the devil, and he will flee from you."*
>
> **James 4:7**

F. Satan will try to get your eyes onto the **physical realm** (emotions, feelings, circumstances) and off the Word of God.

> *"Lord, if its you, Peter replied, tell me to come to you on the water. Come, he said. Then Peter got down out of the boat, walked on the water and came toward Jesus. But when he saw the wind, he was afraid and, beginning to sink, cried out, Lord, save me."*
>
> **Matthew 14:28-30**

G. If he is successful, he will take you captive. **Do not look** at what you can see, but through faith, look at what God has promised and what belongs to you. Let your heart become fully persuaded to the point that you see yourself healed and made whole. God's word will produce vision in your life. There is light at the end of the tunnel. No matter what others are saying, the only report that matters is the report of the Lord. His report says, "*By his stripes ye were healed!*" (**I Peter 2:24**)

> *"While we look not at the things which are seen, but at the things which are not seen: for the things which are seen are temporal; but the things which are not seen are eternal... (For we walk by faith, not by sight:)."*
>
> **2 Corinthians 4:18; 5:7**
>
> *"And Elisha sent a messenger unto him, saying, Go and wash in Jordan seven times, and thy flesh shall come again to thee, and thou shalt be clean. But Naaman was wroth, and went away, and said, Behold, I*

> *thought, He will surely come out to me, and stand, and call on the name of the Lord his God, and strike his hand over the place, and recover the leper."*
>
> **2 Kings 5:10,11**

> **Note**: Don't try to be God or imagine what you would do if you were in charge. This is exactly what satan did in the beginning. Simply take God at His word and He'll bring it to pass in your life. Remember, obedience is the key!)

H. If satan can keep you in the realm of reasoning, he will win all the time. But if you will stay in the realm of faith, then you will defeat him every time because satan is the eternally defeated one. He walks around as a roaring lion seeking whom he may devour, looking for a window of opportunity to come on in. His first port of entry is the mind, which is the battlefield of every believer. (*We looked at this earlier.*) That's why we must weight each thought.

> *"Casting down imaginations, and every high thing that exalteth itself against the knowledge of God, and bringing into captivity every thought to the obedience of Christ."*
>
> **2 Corinthians 10:5**
>
> *"Be well balanced (temperate, sober of mind), be vigilant and cautious at all times; for that enemy of yours, the devil, roams around like a lion roaring [in fierce hunger], seeking someone to seize upon and devour."*
>
> **1 Peter 5:8 (AMP)**

I. Satan wants you to accept the testimony of man; the doctor's report; how you feel or what happened to your friend who had the same thing. But God wants you to accept the testimony of His written Word. Whose report will you believe?

> *"If we receive the witness of men, the witness of God is greater: for this is the witness of God which he hath testified of his Son."*
>
> **1 John 5:9**
>
> *"Who hath believed our report? And to whom is the arm of the LORD revealed?"*
>
> **Isaiah 53:1**

4. God is the deliverer **NOT** the author of sickness.

> *"I am the LORD that healeth thee."*
>
> **Exodus 15:26**
>
> *"Many are the afflictions of the righteous: but the LORD delivereth him out of them all."*
>
> **Psalm 34:19**
>
> *"Bless the LORD, O my soul, and forget not all his benefits: Who forgiveth all thine iniquities; who healeth all thy diseases; Who redeemeth thy life from destruction; who crowneth thee with loving kindness and tender mercies."*
>
> **Psalm 103:2-4**
>
> *"He sent his word, and healed them, and delivered them from their destructions."*
>
> **Psalm 107:20**
>
> *"And it shall come to pass in that day, that his burden shall be taken away from off thy shoulder, and his yoke from off thy neck, and the yoke shall be destroyed because of the anointing."*
>
> **Isaiah 10:27**
>
> *"How God anointed Jesus of Nazareth with the Holy Ghost and with power: who went about doing good, and healing all that were oppressed of the devil; for God was with him."*
>
> **Acts 10:38**
>
> *"For this purpose the Son of God was manifested, that he might destroy the works of the devil."*
>
> **1 John 3:8**

## II. HOW DID SICKNESS AND DISEASE ENTER INTO THE WORLD?

1. Through the fall of man in the Garden of Eden – via sin. God did not create mankind sick. Something happened to mankind as a direct result of his willful disobedience.

> *"And God said, Let us make man in our image, after our likeness: and let them have dominion over the fish of the sea, and over the fowl of the air, and over the cattle, and over all the earth, and over every creeping thing that creepeth upon the earth. So God created man in his own image, in the image*

*of God created he him; male and female created he them."*

**Genesis 1:26,17**

*"And the Lord God took the man, and put him into the garden of Eden to dress it and to keep it. And the Lord God commanded the man, saying, Of every tree of the garden thou mayest freely eat: But of the tree of the knowledge of good and evil, thou shalt not eat of it: for in the day that thou eatest thereof thou shalt surely die."*

**Genesis 2:15-17**

*"For all have sinned, and come short of the glory of God."*

**Romans 3:23**

*"He that committeth sin is of the devil; for the devil sinneth from the beginning. For this purpose the Son of God was manifested, that he might destroy the works of the devil."*

**1 John 3:8**

A. Satan will challenge and undermine your foundation…i.e., the word of God.

- "*Hath God said.*" (Genesis 3:1)
- He will lie to you and try to complicate things
- I Corinthians 11:3 – "*the serpent beguiled Eve through his subtilty.*"
- He will try to reason with you

**EX**: "That not what that really means."
**EX**: "That's spiritual healing not physical healing."
**EX**: "Healing is passed away."

B. Satan will endeavor to cast a shadow on the very character, goodness and motives of God.

**EX**: "God knows if you eat the fruit, you'll be just like Him. You won't really die. God just said that to scare you and to keep you away from the tree."
**EX**: "Remember the last time you prayed…God didn't come through for you. How come? Why did God do this? Why didn't God do that?"

- Many Christians are angry at God and it will hinder their faith.

C. Adam and Eve lost their faith in the integrity of God's word.

> *"And when the woman saw that the tree was good for food, and that it was pleasant to the eyes, and a tree to be desired to make one wise, she took of the fruit thereof, and did eat, and gave also unto her husband with her; and he did eat."*
>
> **Genesis 3:6**

2. Sin was the door through which sickness and disease entered into the world.

> *"Wherefore, as by one man sin entered into the world, and death by sin; and so death passed upon all men, for that all have sinned."*
>
> **Romans 5:12**

3. Sin will open the door in a person's life for sickness and disease to come through.

> *"Afterward Jesus findeth him in the temple, and said unto him, Behold, thou art made whole: sin no more, lest a worse thing come unto thee."*
>
> **John 5:14**
>
> *"Fools because of their transgression, and because of their iniquities, are afflicted."*
>
> **Psalm 107:17**

## III. DOES GOD CREATE SIN AS SOME BELIEVE?

1. No, that would make God a devil. God may permit sin, but He does not create it.

   A. If God commits sin, then He has no right to judge man for sinning.

> *"He did it to demonstrate his justice at the present time, so as to be just and the one who justifies those who have faith in Jesus."*
>
> **Romans 3:26**

   B. Permission is not the same as commission.

> **EX:** A lifeguard at a beach is responsible for patrolling the area between the two flags. If a swimmer chooses to go beyond the boundaries, the lifeguard may allow it, but did not encourage it. The swimmer has now taken his life in his own hands and is responsible for the outcome.

2. God has set certain laws into motion from the beginning of time. One of those laws is the law of reaping as well as the law of sowing. Evil and bad results will come when men sow sin.

> *"Be not deceived; God is not mocked: for whatsoever a man soweth, that shall he also reap. For he that soweth to his flesh shall of the flesh reap corruption; but he that soweth to the Spirit shall of the Spirit reap life everlasting."*
>
> **Galatians 6:7-8**

3. If men sin and reap because of it, it was their responsibility both for their own actions, as well as for the consequences. God simply made the law and the penalties for breaking the law. Men decide their own destiny.

## IV. CONCLUSION

1. God is the liberator; satan is the oppressor. God is a good God and the devil is a mean devil. Remember this and it will help keep your doctrine in order.

2. Keep sin out of your life, and sickness will find no place in you.

3. If we don't like the harvest that we've been eating, then we need to change the seed.

**- Selah -**

# LESSON 2

# IS HEALING FOR ALL?

## I. WHY IS IT THAT SOME PEOPLE ARE HEALED AND SOME ARE NOT? DOES GOD HAVE FAVORITES OR IS HEALING FOR EVERYONE?

1. There are two main roadblocks to Divine Healing, which can be overcome by answering *two* simple questions: Is God able to heal me? And is He willing to heal me now? You must settle these questions once and for all before you can go any further.

> *"The entrance of thy words giveth light; it giveth understanding unto the simple."*
>
> **Psalms 119:130**
>
> *"Jesus Christ the same yesterday, and to day, and for ever."*
>
> **Hebrews 13:8**
>
> *"For I am the Lord, I change not."*
>
> **Malachi 3:6**

2. One of the most popular traditions that the enemy has used to rob Christian's is: "*God may heal some, but it is not His will to heal all.*" If this were true, then God's promises to heal are not for everyone. The only alternative left would be to abandon our Bibles and hope and pray that God has favored us and wants to heal us. This would mean that God's Word is not actually for everyone. Of course this kind of thinking and man-made tradition is nonsense and unscriptural. God's Word has been given to us in order that we might be partakers of His divine nature. Jesus stated that His Word was truth and when we know the truth, the truth shall make us free.

> *"Sanctify them through thy truth: thy word is truth."*
>
> **John 17:17**
>
> *"And ye shall know the truth, and the truth shall make you free."*
>
> **John 8:32**

> *"According as his divine power hath given unto us all things that pertain unto life and godliness, through the knowledge of him that hath called us to glory and virtue: Whereby are given unto us exceeding great and precious promises: that by these ye might be partakers of the divine nature."*
>
> **2 Peter 1:3,4**

3. Much of the church family today believe that healing is based on the will of God, i.e., He wills to heal some and others He doesn't. If you're healed then it was God's will, and if you're not healed then it wasn't God's will.

   A. With this kind of reasoning, human experience becomes the determining factor for healing.

   B. Where did Jesus place the emphasis when it comes to divine healing?
      - On the individuals faith.
      - There are **10** accounts in the Gospels where Jesus *specifically* attributed the persons healing in connection to their faith and not to Jesus' power or faith.

> **Nobleman's son**
> **(John 4:50) –** *"Jesus saith unto him, Go thy way; thy son liveth. And the man believed the word that Jesus had spoken unto him, and he went his way."*
>
> **Paralyzed man through the roof**
> **(Mark 2:5,11) –** *"When Jesus saw their faith, he said unto the sick of the palsy, Son, thy sins be forgiven thee…I say unto thee, Arise, and take up thy bed, and go thy way into thine house."*
>
> **Centurion's servant**
> **(Matthew 8:13) –** *"Go thy way; and as thou hast believed, so be it done unto thee."*
>
> **Jairus**
> **(Mark 5:36) –** *"As soon as Jesus heard the word that was spoken, he saith unto the ruler of the synagogue, Be not afraid, only believe."*
>
> **Woman with the issue of blood**
> **(Mark 5:34) –** *"Daughter, thy faith hath made thee whole."*
>
> **Two blind men**
> **(Matthew 9:29) –** *"According to your faith be it unto you."*

**Canaanite woman's daughter**
**(Matthew 15:28) –** *"O woman, great is thy faith: be it unto thee even as thou wilt."*

**Ten lepers**
**(Luke 17:19) –** *"Arise, go thy way: thy faith hath made thee whole."*

**Blind Bartimaeus**
**(Mark 10:52) –** *"Go thy way; thy faith hath made thee whole."*

**Father's demoniac son**
**(Mark 9:23,24) –** *"Jesus said unto him, If thou canst believe, all things are possible to him that believeth. And straightway the father of the child cried out, and said with tears, Lord, I believe; help thou mine unbelief."*

**Note:** The determining factor was faith. Some believe and others do not. This is what determines if you are saved or healed. (**Romans 10:9,10**)

4. In **John 14:14**, Jesus declared, *"If you shall ask anything in my name I will do it."* Anything would have to include healing because He did not omit healing from this promise. Over in **John 15:7**, Jesus said, *"If you abide in me, and my words abide in you, ye shall ask what ye will, and it shall be done unto you."* Notice, *"You shall ask what YOU will"* would have to also include healing because he did not exclude it. In **John 16:23**, Jesus said, *"Whatsoever ye shall ask the Father in my name, he will give it you."* Healing would have to be included in the whatsoever because He never specifically left it out.

5. In **Mark 11:24**, Jesus stated that, *"What things soever ye desire, when ye pray, believe that ye receive them, and ye shall have them."* Notice that Jesus never did quality this statement with the exclusion of healing. If He did, it might have sounded like this. "*What things soever ye desire, this does not include healing, when ye pray, believe that ye receive them, with the exception of healing, and ye shall have them.*" Since Jesus did not exclude healing, then healing would have to be included in the *"what things soever ye desire"* in order for this promise to be valid.

6. There will be those who fail to receive healing today, but it's never because it wasn't God's will to heal them. God is not a respecter of persons, but He is a rewarder of faith. He never turned faith away empty handed. All who came in faith were healed.

> *"God is no respecter of persons."*
>
> **Acts 10:34**
>
> *"For there is no respect of persons with God."*
>
> **Romans 2:11**
>
> *"And, ye masters, do the same things unto them, forbearing threatening: knowing that your Master also is in heaven; neither is there respect of persons with him."*
>
> **Ephesians 6:9**
>
> *"But without faith it is impossible to please him: for he that cometh to God must believe that he is, and that he is a rewarder of them that diligently seek him."*
>
> **Hebrews 11:6**

7. In **Matthew 17:14-21**, we find the story of a demon-possessed boy whom the disciples were trying to set free, after his father had brought him to them. After their unsuccessful attempt, they brought the boy to Jesus who then in turn instantly healed and set him free. Jesus proved it was still God's will to heal even those who fail to receive healing and noted the failure was the disciple's unbelief as well as the fathers. (Compare **Mk 9:14-29**)

8. Unbelief will stop the flow of the anointing every time.

> *"And he could there do no mighty work, save that he laid his hands upon a few sick folk, and healed them. And he marveled because of their unbelief."*
> **Mark 6:5-6**

9. If sickness is the will of God, then why do we have doctors and hospitals? If sickness is the will of God, then any attempt to get well through medical assistance would be in direct rebellion to the will of God. But what's the first thing that most folks do when they're not feeling good? They make a doctors appointment. If sickness is the will of God, then we why do we support medical science and not close it down. If you really believe that sickness is God's will for you, then ask God for a double portion of the sickness so you can stay in the center of His will. No, thank God for medical science. It may help you stay alive long enough until your faith can lay hold of God's best.

10. I've noticed that many people make a lot of statements based on human experience rather than basing their statements on the Word of God. You see this is where people miss it. We must never bring the Word of God down to the level of human experience. God's Word is true whether we experience his best or not.

**EX:** "Uncle Bill died of cancer and he was a Christian. If anybody should have been healed, it should have been Uncle Bill. After all, he was the pastor for the last 25 years."

A. Is healing based on what happens to Uncle Bill? Or is healing based on what Jesus did for Uncle Bill 2000 years ago at Calvary?

B. You cannot change history. History records that Jesus exchanged places with you and when He did He healed you.

C. Some say that, "*In His time he'll heal me.*" Friend, God's time was 2000 years ago at Calvary.

> *"Surely he hath borne our griefs, and carried our sorrows: yet we did esteem him stricken, smitten of God, and afflicted. But he was wounded for our transgressions, he was bruised for our iniquities: the chastisement of our peace was upon him; and with his stripes we are healed."*
>
> **Isaiah 53:4-5**
>
> *"Bless the LORD, O my soul, and forget not all his benefits: Who forgiveth all thine iniquities; who healeth all thy diseases."*
>
> **Psalm 103:2-3**

11. If it's not God's will to heal you then why did He?

> *"Who his own self bare our sins in his own body on the tree, that we, being dead to sins, should live unto righteousness: by whose stripes ye were healed."*
>
> **1 Peter 2:24**

12. **Ephesians 1:22** tells us that the church is the body of Christ. Does God want the body of Christ sick, diseased and bedridden? Isn't God's will to heal the whole body and every member in it or does He only heal certain parts of His body? If healing was only for exclusive members of His body, why does he command "*any sick*" in it to be anointed for healing? Any would have to include you wouldn't it? If you were not included that would mean that God has favorites. If He has favorites, this would violate His very own word, in which case why should we or how could we believe anything else to be true in the bible?

> *"Is any sick among you? Let him call for the elders of the church; and let them pray over him, anointing him with oil in the name of the Lord: And the prayer of faith shall save the sick, and the Lord shall raise him up; and if he have committed sins, they shall be forgiven him. Confess your faults one to another, and pray one for another, that ye may be healed. The effectual fervent prayer of a righteous man availeth much."*
>
> **James 5:14-16**

13. There are still those who have never heard the Gospel. There is a harvest that needs to be reached. In order for this to happen, God needs willing vessels; those who say, "Lord here I am, send me." In light of this, how do you suppose we can fulfill the great commission if we're home sick and in bed. **Romans 12:1** tells us that we are to present our bodies as a living sacrifice unto God. What kind of a body do you think the Lord would rather prefer in the vineyard? A weak and sickly body or a strong and healthy body? Which one would be more effective for Kingdom business? Which one would be more effective in reaching the lost?

14. **Hebrews 13:8** states that, *"Jesus Christ the same yesterday, and today, and for ever."* This means that if He ever had the compassion and ability to heal the sick yesterday, He has the same compassion and ability to heal the sick today. If He is not moved with compassion to heal today, then He has changed. We know that is not possible because **Malachi 3:6** states, "*I am the Lord, I change not.*"

15. The Bible tells us that right now we live under a better covenant with better promises. We're living in the dispensation of Grace. Under the old covenant, those who were afflicted were able to reach out and be healed by a merciful and compassionate God. Is the Lord no longer merciful or full of compassion to those who would reach out to Him for healing under the new covenant? Has God changed?

> *"But now hath he obtained a more excellent ministry, by how much also he is the mediator of a better covenant, which was established upon better promises."*
>
> **Hebrews 8:6**

16. There are those who believe that God has other means for us to be healed today outside of divine healing. Yes it's true that in many cases there are other means outside of divine healing where a person can get well. But if this were God's best, then why would God implement a less successful method under the new and better covenant?

> **EX**: "Try this and see if it helps. If not, make another appointment and I'll give you something else to try."
> **EX**: "It's a very delicate operation. But I would still give him a 50/50 chance of pulling through it. There are no promises, but let's keep our fingers crossed."

17. During His earthly ministry, Jesus was the will of God in action. He stated himself that what He sees the Father do, that is what He does too. Therefore when Jesus healed all the sick who came to Him, this was a revelation of the will of God for our bodies.

> *"Then answered Jesus and said unto them, Verily, verily, I say unto you, The Son can do nothing of himself, but what he seeth the Father do: for what things soever he doeth, these also doeth the Son likewise."*
>
> **John 5:19**

18. Jesus stated in **John 14:12-14** that believers would continue His work on the earth as they go forth in His name. What was the work of Christ? As you study Jesus' earthly ministry, you'll discover it was three-fold: Preaching, teaching and healing all manner of sickness and disease. Reach John 14:12-14 and ask yourself this: "Do you believe when Jesus made this statement he was telling the truth? Do you believe when Jesus made this statement He knew what He was talking about?" If so, imagine how much confidence this should give to every believer who goes forth in the power of His name.

> *"And Jesus went about all Galilee, teaching in their synagogues, and preaching the gospel of the kingdom, and healing all manner of sickness and all manner of disease among the people."*
>
> **Matthew 4:23**
>
> *"Verily, verily, I say unto you, He that believeth on me, the works that I do shall he do also; and greater works than these shall he do; because I go unto my Father. And whatsoever ye shall ask in my name, that will I do, that the Father may be glorified in the Son. If ye shall ask any thing in my name, I will do it."*
>
> **John 14:12-14**

19. The book of Acts reveals to us the way that Jesus wants to continue to move through the Church. Jesus has empowered the church for the miraculous when He sent the Holy Spirit on the Day of Pentecost. The Holy Spirit simply continues the same works of Jesus today through the Church. Notice how the disciples prayed and what

type of response which they had as they went forth in His name.

> *"And now, Lord, behold their threatenings: and grant unto thy servants, that with all boldness they may speak thy word, By stretching forth thine hand to heal; and that signs and wonders may be done by the name of thy holy child Jesus. And when they had prayed, the place was shaken where they were assembled together; and they were all filled with the Holy Ghost, and they spake the word of God with boldness. And the multitude of them that believed were of one heart and of one soul: neither said any of them that ought of the things which he possessed was his own; but they had all things common. And with great power gave the apostles witness of the resurrection of the Lord Jesus: and great grace was upon them all."*
>
> **Acts 4:29-33**

20. **Galatians 3:13** states that, *"Christ hath redeemed us from the curse of the law, being made a curse for us: for it is written, Cursed is every one that hangeth on a tree."* The curse of the Law was three-fold: poverty, sickness and spiritual death. If we've been redeemed by the blood of the Lamb from the curse of the law, and all its effects, then why would God expect you to remain under the curse when Jesus was made a curse for you?

21. In **1 John 3:8**, we are told that, *"The Son of God was manifested that He might destroy the works of the devil."* Sickness and disease are the works of the devil. **(Acts 10:38)** Would God want the works of the devil to remain in your body, which by the way is the temple of the Holy Ghost? Of course not, that's why He came to destroy them!

> *"Know ye not that your bodies are the members of Christ? What? know ye not that your body is the temple of the Holy Ghost which is in you, which ye have of God, and ye are not your own? For ye are bought with a price: therefore glorify God in your body, and in your spirit, which are God's."*
>
> **1 Corinthians 6:15,19-20**

22. If God is willing to show forgiveness to His enemies, surely He is equally as willing to show healing to His sons and daughters. Would you do any less for your child?

> *"He that spared not his own Son, but delivered him up for us all, how shall he not with him also freely give us all things?"*
>
> **Romans 8:32**
>
> *"If ye then, being evil, know how to give good gifts unto your children, how much more shall your Father which is in heaven give good things to them that ask him?"*
>
> **Matthew 7:11**

23. In the Gospels when Jesus commissioned the disciples to preach the Gospel, He also commanded them to heal the sick. The Gospel is good news to a sick person. The fact that Jesus bore your sickness and disease means that you can be healed. The message the early church preached always caused faith to rise up in the hearts of the listeners and gave them hope that their situation can change.

> *"And as ye go, preach, saying, The kingdom of heaven is at hand. Heal the sick, cleanse the lepers, raise the dead, cast out devils: freely ye have received, freely give."*
>
> **Matthew 10:7,8**
>
> *"Then he called his twelve disciples together, and gave them power and authority over all devils, and to cure diseases. And he sent them to preach the kingdom of God, and to heal the sick."*
>
> **Luke 9:1,2**
>
> *"And into whatsoever city ye enter, and they receive you, eat such things as are set before you: And heal the sick that are therein, and say unto them, The kingdom of God is come nigh unto you."*
>
> **Luke 10:8,9**

24. In **Romans 10:17**, the Word of God tells us that, *"faith cometh by hearing and hearing by the Word of God."* How could faith for healing come by hearing the Word of God, if God never promised it or made provision for it? If there is no hope or good news for the sick to hear, then there is nothing for them to believe. If there is nothing for the to believe, then they will not be calling on the name of the Lord. The fact is that there is healing in the word. There is hope for the hopeless. God's word is medicine or health to our bodies.

> *"Bless the LORD, O my soul, and forget not all his benefits: Who forgiveth all thine iniquities; who healeth all thy diseases."*
>
> **Psalm 103:2-3**
>
> *"My son, attend to my words; incline thine ear unto my sayings. Let them not depart from thine eyes; keep them in the midst of thine heart. For they are life unto those that find them, and health to all their flesh."*
>
> **Proverbs 4:20-23**

25. According to **Acts 2:21**, *"Whosoever shall call upon the name of the Lord shall be saved."* The Greek word for saved is the word "*sozo*," which happens to be the all-inclusive word meaning: protection; safety, to heal, to make whole and restore to health. Keeping

this in mind, remember that the Gospel is open to "*whosoever will*" and that would certainly include you. You can receive your healing right now. The Lord has never changed. He's still loving, forgiving, caring and His healing power is available for you right now. Call on Him!

> *"And whosoever will, let him take the water of life freely."*
>
> **Revelation 22:17**
>
> *"Neither is there salvation in any other: for there is none other name under heaven given among men, whereby we must be saved (sozo)."*
>
> **Acts 4:12**

## II. CONCLUSION

1. God is not a respecter of persons but He is a rewarder of faith.

2. Faith is the ingredient that will release the healing power of God in your life and in your sick body.

3. God has never changed. He healed yesterday, He is healing today and He will heal tomorrow.

> *"For I am the Lord, I change not."*
>
> **Malachi 3:6**
>
> *"Jesus Christ the same yesterday, and to day, and for ever."*
>
> **Hebrews 13:8**
>
> *"I will not violate my covenant or alter what my lips have uttered."*
>
> **Psalm 89:34 (NIV)**

**- Selah -**

# LESSON 3

# HE HEALED EVERYONE

## I. HEALING EVERY ONE

1. **Matthew 4:23-24** *"And Jesus went about all Galilee, teaching in their synagogues, and preaching the gospel of the kingdom, and healing all manner of sickness and all manner of disease among the people. And his fame went throughout all Syria: and they brought unto him all sick people that were taken with diverse diseases and torments, and those which were possessed with devils, and those which were lunatick, and those that had the palsy; and he healed them."*

2. **Matthew 8:16** *"When the even was come, they brought unto him many that were possessed with devils: and he cast out the spirits with his word, and healed all that were sick."*

3. **Matthew 9:35-10:1** *"And Jesus went about all the cities and villages, teaching in their synagogues, and preaching the gospel of the kingdom, and healing every sickness and every disease among the people. But when he saw the multitudes, he was moved with compassion on them, because they fainted, and were scattered abroad, as sheep having no shepherd. Then saith he unto his disciples, The harvest truly is plenteous, but the labourers are few. Pray ye therefore the Lord of the harvest, that he will send forth labourers into his harvest. And when he had called unto him his twelve disciples, he gave them power against unclean spirits, to cast them out, and to heal all manner of sickness and all manner of disease."*

4. **Matthew 11:4-5** *"Jesus answered and said unto them, Go and shew John again those things which ye do hear and see: The blind receive their sight, and the lame walk, the lepers are cleansed, and the deaf hear, the dead are raised up, and the poor have the gospel preached to them."*

5. **Matthew 12:15** *"But when Jesus knew it, he withdrew himself from there: and great multitudes followed him, and he healed them all."*

6. **Matthew 14:13-14** *"When Jesus heard of it, he departed thence by ship into a desert place apart: and when the people had heard thereof, they followed him on foot out of the cities. And Jesus went forth, and saw a great multitude, and was moved with compassion toward them, and he healed their sick."*

7. **Matthew 14:34-36** *"And when they were gone over, they came into* the *land of Gennesaret. And when the men of that place had knowledge of him, they sent out into all that country round about, and brought unto him all that were diseased; And besought him that they might only touch the hem of his garment and as many as touched were made perfectly whole."* (Mark 6:54-56)

8. **Matthew 15:30-31** *"And great multitudes came unto him, having with them those that were lame, blind, dumb, maimed, and many others, and cast them down at Jesus' feet; and he healed them: Insomuch that the multitude wondered, when they saw the dumb to speak, the maimed to be whole, the lame to walk, and the blind to see: and they glorified the God of Israel."*

9. **Matthew 19:1-2** *"And it came to pass, that when Jesus had finished these sayings, he departed from Galilee, and came into the coasts of Judaea beyond Jordan; And great multitudes followed him; and he healed them there."*

10. **Matthew 21:13-14** *"And said unto them, It is written, My house shall be called the house of prayer; but ye have made it a den of thieves. And the blind and the lame came to him in the temple; and he healed them."*

11. **Mark 6:54-56** *"And when they were come out of the ship, straight-way they knew him, And ran through that whole region round about, and began to carry about in beds those that were sick, where they heard he was. And whithersoever he entered, into villages, or cities, or country, they laid the sick in the streets, and besought him that they might touch if it were but the border of his garment: and as many as touched him were made whole."* (Matthew 14:34)

12. **Luke 4:40** *"Now when the sun was setting, all they that had any sick with divers diseases brought them unto him; and he laid his hands on every one of them, and healed them."*

13. **Luke 6:17-19** *"And he came down with them, and stood in the plain, and the company of his disciples, and a great multitude of people out of all Judaea and Jerusalem, and from the sea coast of Tyre and Sidon, which came to hear him, and to be healed of their diseases; And they that were vexed with unclean spirits: and they were healed. And the whole multitude sought to touch him: for there went virtue out of him, and healed them all."*

14. **Luke 9:10,11** *"And the apostles, when they were returned, told him all that they had done. And he took them, and went aside privately into a desert place belonging to the city called Bethsaida. And the people, when they knew it, followed him: and he received them, and spake unto them of the kingdom of God, and healed them that had need of healing."* (Matthew 14:13)

**Note:** Notice that in every single one of these healings, they all happened under the Old Covenant. The New Covenant did not come into being until Jesus' death, burial, and resurrection. Every person Jesus ministered to, He ministered to under the Old

Covenant. And everyone under the Old Covenant who came to Jesus could get healed, Keep in mind the fact that none of them were born-again, or Spirit-filled, but were Israelites looking for the Messiah. They couldn't be born-again until after Jesus' death, burial, resurrection and ascension. From a spiritual standpoint they were sinners. Here's the thing: If everyone of them that came could get healed, and we have a better covenant **(Hebrews 8:6)**, established upon better promises; on top of that, we've been redeemed by the blood of Jesus and filled with the Holy Ghost. If we can't get healed then the New Covenant is not as good as the Old Covenant. In order for the New Covenant to be better than the Old Covenant, it has to contain everything that the Old Covenant has and more, or else it's not as good. It couldn't be better if it doesn't at least have what the Old one had - and under the Old, everybody could get healed.

15. **Acts 5:15,16** *"Insomuch that they brought forth the sick into the streets, and laid them on beds and couches, that at the least the shadow of Peter passing by might overshadow some of them. There came also a multitude out of the cities round about unto Jerusalem, bringing sick folks, and them which were vexed with unclean spirits: and they were healed every one."*

16. **Acts 28:8,9** *"And it came to pass, that the father of Publius lay sick of a fever and of a bloody flux: to whom Paul entered in, and prayed, and laid his hands on him, and healed him. So when this was done, others also, which had diseases in the island, came, and were healed."*

## II. IF UNDER THE OLD COVENANT IT WAS GOD'S WILL TO HEAL ONLY SOME AND NOT ALL, THEN HOW DID THE PEOPLE KNOW WHICH ONES TO BRING TO JESUS TO BE HEALED?

1. The Gospels tell us that Jesus healed them all!

2. Jesus never refused to heal anyone who came to him for healing.

3. Jesus' healing power was available to anyone who would receive it.

4. God is not a respecter of person's, but He is a rewarder of faith.

> *"But without faith it is impossible to please him: for he that cometh to God must believe that he is, and that he is a rewarder of them that diligently seek him."*
>
> **Hebrews 11:6**

5. Jesus' healing power is available to you right now.

> *"Jesus Christ the same yesterday, and to day, and for ever."*
>
> **Hebrews 13:8**

## III. CONCLUSION

1. You have not because you ask not.

> *"Ask, and it shall be given you; seek, and ye shall find; knock, and it shall be opened unto you: For every one that asketh receiveth; and he that seeketh findeth; and to him that knocketh it shall be opened."*
>
> **Matthew 7:7,8**

2. Jesus is the will of God in action - healing every one who came to him in faith.

> *"He is the sole expression of the glory of God [the Light- being, the out-raying or radiance of the divine], and He is the perfect imprint and very image of [Gods] nature, upholding and maintaining and guiding and propelling the universe by His mighty word of power."*
>
> **Hebrews 1:3 (AMP)**
>
> *"And besought him that they might only touch the hem of his garment: and as many as touched were made perfectly whole."*
>
> **Matthew 14:36**

3. Too many Christians are waiting for God to do something about their illness, not realizing that He's already made the provision through the Lord Jesus Christ. It's up to us to accept His provision. Will you be healed?

> *"I pray that the sharing of your faith may become effective as you fully acknowledge every blessing that is ours in Christ."*
>
> **Philemon 1:6 (ISV)**
>
> *"Bless the LORD, O my soul, and forget not all his benefits: Who forgiveth all thine iniquities; who healeth all thy diseases; Who redeemeth thy life from destruction; who crowneth thee with loving kindness and tender mercies."*
>
> **Psalm 103:2-4**

**- Selah -**

# LESSON 4

# ARE MIRACLES FOR TODAY?

## I. WERE MIRACLES AND HEALINGS ONLY UNDER THE OLD COVENANT? IS GOD STILL A MIRACLE WORKING GOD?

One of the most common traditions that has circulated throughout the church world is that, "*The age of miracles is past.*" The myth is that when the last apostle died the age of miracles ceased, hence God doesn't work miracles anymore. In order for this to be true, then miracles would have to be nonexistent. If just one miracle occurs, then that "theory" goes right out the window. If the age of miracles is over, then how do we explain all the medically documented cases of miraculous healings? As for me personally, I have witnessed hundreds of miracles of all kinds around the world such as the dear hearing, the dumb speaking, the blind seeing, tumors disappearing and more.

A. The question we need to be asking is: "What does the bible say?" Not what does our church believe? Not what does our pastor teach? Neither should we follow any of our church traditions that are contrary to God's word. Did miracles occur in the new covenant outside of those which Jesus did? Meditate on the following verses.

1. **Malachi 3:6** *"For I am the LORD, I change not."* (Then He's still Jehovah Rapha!)

2. **Hebrews 8:6** *"He is the mediator of a better covenant, which was established upon better promises."* (If God healed under the old covenant, then He must still heal under the new because it's even better. No more sacrifices to bring to the priests, Jesus was the ultimate sacrifice once and for all.)

3. **Hebrews 13:8** *"Jesus Christ the same yesterday, and today, and for ever."*

4. **Mark 9:23** *"Jesus said unto him, If thou canst believe, all things are possible to him that believeth."*

5. **John 14:12-14** *"Verily, verily, I say unto you, He that believeth on me, the works that I do shall he do also; and greater works than these shall he do; because I go unto my Father. And*

*whatsoever ye shall ask in my name, that will I do, that the Father may be glorified in the Son. If ye shall ask anything in my name, I will do it."*

6. **Romans 8:11** *"But if the Spirit of him that raised up Jesus from the dead dwell in you, he that raised up Christ from the dead shall also quicken* (give life to) *your mortal bodies by his Spirit that dwelleth in you."* (Nothing is too difficult for God to heal, restore or replace.)

7. **Galatians 3:29** *"And if ye be Christ's, then are ye Abraham's seed, and heirs according to the promise."* What promise? **(Exodus 23:25,26)** *"And ye shall serve the LORD your God, and he shall bless thy bread, and thy water; and I will take sickness away from the midst of thee. There shall nothing cast their young, nor be barren, in thy land: the number of thy days I will fulfill."*

8. **Ephesians 1:3** *"Blessed be the God and Father of our Lord Jesus Christ, who hath blessed us with all spiritual blessings in heavenly places in Christ."* (Then it must to include healing.)

9. **Acts 3:1-8** *"Now Peter and John went up together into the temple at the hour of prayer, being the ninth hour. And a certain man lame from his mother's womb was carried, whom they laid daily at the gate of the temple which is called Beautiful, to ask alms of them that entered into the temple; Who seeing Peter and John about to go into the temple asked an alms. And Peter, fastening his eyes upon him with John, said, Look on us. And he gave heed unto them expecting to receive something of them. Then Peter said, silver and gold have I none; but such as I have give I thee: In the name of Jesus Christ of Nazareth rise up and walk. And he took him by the right hand, and lifted him up: and immediately his feet and ankle bones received strength. And he leaping up stood, and walked, and entered with them into the temple, walking, and leaping, and praising God."*

**Note**: Keep in mind as we read Acts that these events are happening under the new covenant, which now has been ratified by the blood of Jesus.

10. **Acts 4:29-33** *"And now, Lord, behold their threatening's: and grant unto thy servants, that with all boldness they may speak thy word, By stretching forth thine hand to heal; and that signs and wonders may be done by the name of thy holy child Jesus. And when they had prayed, the place was shaken where they were assembled together; and they were all filled with the Holy Ghost, and they spake the word of God with boldness. And the multitude of them that believed were of one heart and of one soul: neither said any of them that ought of the things which he possessed was his own; but they had all things common. And with great power gave the apostles witness of the resurrection of the Lord Jesus: and great grace was upon them all."*

11. **Acts 5:12-16** *"And by the hands of the apostles were many signs and wonders wrought among the people; (and they were all with one accord in Solomon's porch. And of the rest durst no man join himself to them: but the people magnified them. And believers were the more added to the Lord, multitudes both of men and women.) Insomuch that they brought forth the sick into the streets, and laid them on beds and couches, that at the least the shadow of Peter passing by might overshadow some of them. There came also a multitude out of the cities round about unto Jerusalem, bringing sick folks, and them which were vexed with unclean spirits: and they were healed every one."*

12. **Acts 6:7** *"And Stephen, full of faith and power, did great wonders and miracles among the people."* (Stephen was not an apostle, and yet look how God used him.)

13. **Acts 8:5-8** *"Then Philip went down to the city of Samaria, and preached Christ unto them. And the people with one accord gave heed unto those things which Philip spake, hearing and seeing the miracles, which he did. For unclean spirits, crying with loud voice, came out of many that were possessed with them: and many taken with palsies, and that were lame, were healed. And there was great joy in that city."* (Philip was not an apostle either, but this did not stop God from healing folks or delivering them.)

14. **Acts 9:32-34** *"And it came to pass, as Peter passed throughout all quarters, he came down also to the saints which dwelt at Lydda. And there he found a certain man named Aeneas, which had kept his bed eight years, and was sick of the palsy. And Peter said unto him, Aeneas, Jesus Christ maketh thee whole: arise, and make thy bed. And he arose immediately."*

15. **Acts 9:36-41** *"Now there was at Joppa a certain disciple named Tabitha, which by interpretation is called Dorcas: this woman was full of good works and almsdeeds which she did. And it came to pass in those days, that she was sick, and died…And forasmuch as Lydda was nigh to Joppa, and the disciples had heard that Peter was there, they sent unto him two men, desiring him that he would not delay to come to them. Then Peter arose and went with them…and prayed; and turning him to the body said, Tabitha, arise. And she opened her eyes: and when she saw Peter, she sat up. And he gave her his hand, and lifted her up, and when he had called the saints and widows, presented her alive."*

16. **Acts 14:3** *"Long time therefore abode they speaking boldly in the Lord, which gave testimony unto the word of his grace, and granted signs and wonders to be done by their hands."*

17. **<u>Acts 14:8-10</u>** *"And there sat a certain man at Lystra, impotent in his feet, being a cripple from his mother's womb, who never had walked: The same heard Paul speak: who steadfastly beholding him, and perceiving that he had faith to be healed, Said with a loud voice, stand upright on thy feet. And he leaped and walked."* (Remember that Paul was not one of the original 12 apostles, but this didn't hinder the healing power of God from flowing.)

18. **<u>Acts 16:16-18</u>** *"And it came to pass, as we went to prayer, a certain damsel possessed with a spirit of divination met us, which brought her masters much gain by soothsaying: The same followed Paul and us, and cried, saying, these men are the servants of the most high God, which shew unto us the way of salvation. And this did she many days. But Paul, being grieved, turned and said to the spirit, I command thee in the name of Jesus Christ to come out of her. And he came out the same hour."*

19. **<u>Acts 19:10-12</u>** *"And this continued by the space of two years; so that all they which dwelt in Asia heard the word of the Lord Jesus, both Jews and Greeks. And God wrought special miracles by the hands of Paul: So that from his body were brought unto the sick handkerchiefs or aprons, and the diseases departed from them, and the evil spirits went out of them."*

20. **<u>Acts 28:8,9</u>** *"And it came to pass, that the father of Publius lay sick of a fever and of a bloody flux: to whom Paul entered in, and prayed, and laid his hands on him, and healed him. So when this was done, others also, which had diseases in the island, came, and were healed."*

21. **<u>James 5:14-16</u>** *"Is any sick among you? Let him call for the elders of the church; and let them pray over him, anointing him with oil in the name of the Lord: And the prayer of faith shall save the sick, and the Lord shall raise him up; and if he have committed sins, they shall be forgiven him. Confess your faults one to another, and pray one for another, that ye may be healed. The effectual fervent prayer of a righteous man availeth much."*

22. **<u>1 John 5:14-15</u>** *"And this is the confidence that we have in him, that, if we ask any thing according to his will, he heareth us: And if we know that he hear us, whatsoever we ask, we know that we have the petitions that we desired of him."*

23. **<u>3 John 1:2</u>** *"Beloved, I wish above all things that thou mayest prosper and be in health, even as thy soul prospereth."*

## II. THE GREAT COMMSION HASN'T BEEN REVOKED OR FULFILLED SO THE AGE OF MIRACLES CANNOT BE OVER.

> *"And he said unto them, Go ye into all the world, and preach the gospel to every creature. He that believeth and is baptized shall be saved; but he that believeth not shall be damned. And these signs shall follow them that believe; In my name shall they cast out devils; they shall speak with new tongues; They shall take up serpents; and if they drink any deadly thing, it shall not hurt them; they shall lay hands on the sick, and they shall recover. So then after the Lord had spoken unto them, he was received up into heaven, and sat on the right hand of God. And they went forth, and preached every where, the Lord working with them, and confirming the word with signs following."*
>
> **Mark 16:15-20**

1. Praying for the sick is part of the great commission.

2. Praying for the sick is not exclusive for the apostle or even the 5-fold ministry. The only qualification is that you must be a believer.

3. Expecting results from healing prayers is something that Jesus promised.

4. If healing and miracles were not part of the new covenant, then why would Jesus commission believers to lay hands on the sick to begin with?

5. Until the Lord returns, we are still to go forth in His name preaching the gospel.

6. Healing and deliverance is good news to those who are in need of it.

7. God still demonstrates his goodness today by manifesting His healing power.

8. God works with and confirms with His word, which releases healing to those who embrace it.

## III. CONCLUSION

1. If the day of miracles were over, that would mean God has changed, and we know that the Lord changes not.

> *"For I am the Lord, I change not."*
>
> **Malachi 3:6**

2. We are to continue the ministry of Jesus Christ in this earth through teaching, preaching, and healing the sick in His name.

> *"Verily, verily, I say unto you, He that believeth on me, the works that I do shall he do also; and greater works than these shall he do; because I go unto my Father. And whatsoever ye shall ask in my name, that will I do, that the Father may be glorified in the Son. If ye shall ask any thing in my name, I will do it."*
>
> **John 14:12-14**

3. God still heals through his believers today as they lay hands on the sick in the name of Jesus.

> *"They shall lay hands on the sick, and they shall recover."*
>
> **Mark 16:18**

4. The miraculous opens the door to harvest. It doesn't save people but gets them very much interested in the message of Christ.

> *"And the people with one accord gave heed unto those things which Philip spake, hearing and seeing the miracles which he did."*
>
> **Acts 8:6**

**- Selah -**

# LESSON 5

# HEALING IN THE ATONEMENT

## I. THE DAY OF ATONEMENT (LEVITUCUS 16)

**Note**: The question to answer in this lesson is: Did Jesus redeem us from our diseases when He atoned for our sins? If the answer is yes, then healing is a forever settled subject.

1. The most important day of the year in the Hebrew calendar is the day of Atonement. It is also referred to as "Yom Kippur." In **Leviticus 16:31** it is referred to as "*a Sabbath of rest.*" This was the day when the High Priest entered into the Holy of Holies, the inner most part of the tabernacle, on behalf of the people. He brought with him the blood from the sin offering, which he sprinkled seven times on and before the mercy seat.

> *"And he shall take of the blood of the bullock, and sprinkle it with his finger upon the mercy seat eastward; and before the mercy seat shall he sprinkle of the blood with his finger seven times."*
>
> **Leviticus 16:14**

2. In the Old Testament, the word atonement (Hebrew: Kaphar) has the Hebrew meanings of: to cover, purge, or pardon. Kaphar was first used in **Genesis 6:14,** when Noah "*pitched or covered*" the ark. (**Note**: a type of substance smeared over the boat to waterproof it.)

> *"Make thee an ark of gopher wood; rooms shalt thou make in the ark, and shalt pitch it within and without with pitch."*
>
> **Genesis 6:14**

3. In theology, atonement is a term that embraces the entire sacrificial and redemptive work of Christ. All the offerings offered up by the Levitical priests could not remove or take away the sins of the people, but simply covered their sins until the cross when Christ would come and redeem mankind by shedding His very own blood.

> *"For it is not possible that the blood of bulls and of goats should take away sins."*
>
> **Hebrews 10:4**

4. Because the sins of the people were simply *covered* and *not removed*, by the Levitical sacrifices which were offered up, God only *passed over* them until His righteousness was fully executed through the cross. In other words, the cross was the most violent expression of the righteousness of God. Keep in mind that according to Hebrews 9:22, "*Without the shedding of blood, there is no remission.*" Remember that it was Jesus' blood, not the animal sacrifices, which purchased our eternal redemption.

> *"For God sent Christ Jesus to take the punishment for our sins and to end all God's anger against us. He used Christ's blood and our faith as the means of saving us from his wrath. In this way he was being entirely fair, even though he did not punish those who sinned in former times. For he was looking forward to the time when Christ would come and take away those sins."*
>
> **Romans 3:25 (TLB)**

5. The Order Of The Ceremony was as follows:

   A. First, atonement would be made for the high priest and his family with a sin offering.

   > *"And Aaron shall offer his bullock of the sin offering, which is for himself, and make an atonement for himself, and for his house."*
   >
   > **Leviticus 16:6**

   B. Second, atonement was made for the sins of the people by way of a sin offering.

   > *"Then shall he kill the goat of the sin offering, that is for the people."*
   >
   > **Leviticus 16:15**

   - Two goats were used as a substitute taking the place of the people.
   - One goat was used as the sin offering for the people.
   - The second goat was used as the scapegoat sent off into the wilderness symbolically carrying or removing the sins of the people.
   - The priest would lay both hands on the scapegoat and confess all the sins and wickedness of the people and then release the goat into the wilderness to die. This was a type and shadow of Jesus who one day would come and carry away the sins of humanity outside of the city and die as our substitute.

> *"And Aaron shall lay both his hands upon the head of the live goat, and confess over him all the iniquities of the children of Israel, and all their transgressions in all their sins, putting them upon the head of the goat, and shall send him away by the hand of a fit man into the wilderness: And the goat shall bear upon him all their iniquities unto a land not inhabited: and he shall let go the goat in the wilderness."*
>
> **Leviticus 16:21,22**

C. Finally, the high priest offered up burnt offerings for both himself and the people and concluded by burning the fat from the sin offering.

> *"Then he shall come out and sacrifice the burnt offering for himself and the burnt offering for the people, to make atonement for himself and for the people. He shall also burn the fat of the sin offering on the altar."*
>
> **Leviticus 16:24,25**

D. Remember that this statute or event was yearly. It never had the ability to cleanse a man's conscience or remove his sin. (*The gifts and sacrifices being offered were not able to clear the conscience of the worshiper.*) Hebrews 9:9 (NIV) It only temporarily satisfied the courts of heaven for a season until such a time that God would send forth His very own son as the Lamb who was slain from the foundation of the world. Whatever the cost, God was willing to reach that far in anticipation of redeeming mankind.

## II. JESUS CHRIST IS OUR SACRIFICE AND HIGH PRIEST

1. Just as sin had consequences and demanded a sacrifice under the old covenant, which was carried out by the high priest, likewise sin also demanded a sacrifice under the new covenant.

> *"Whom God hath set forth to be a propitiation through faith in his blood, to declare his righteousness for the remission of sins that are past, through the forbearance of God; To declare, I say, at this time his righteousness: that he might be just, and the justifier of him which believeth in Jesus."*
>
> **Romans 3:25,26**
>
> *"God presented him as a sacrifice of atonement, through faith in his blood. He did this to demonstrate his justice, because in his forbearance he had left the sins committed beforehand unpunished – he did it to demonstrate his justice at the present time, so as to be just and the one who justifies those who have*

*faith in Jesus."*

**Romans 3:25,26 (NIV)**

**<u>Note</u>:** Notice the word "propitiation" used in verse 25. In the Greek, it's the word *hilasterion*. It means to atone for, to appease or expiate. In fact it is the equivalent for the Hebrew word "*kapar*" which means to cover or covering, and refers to the lid of the Ark of the Covenant, i.e., the mercyseat. On the day of atonement the priest would offer the blood sacrifice of an animal and sprinkle it on the mercy seat to atone for the sins of the people, whereby satisfying and appeasing God. This word, *hilasterion* is a picture of God's grace whereby Jesus blood would not only be the covering for our sin, as the mercyseat, but also would be the ultimate sacrifice and payment for sin one and for all.

*"For this reason Christ is the mediator of a new covenant, that those who are called may receive the promised eternal inheritance – now that he has died as a ransom to set them free from the sins committed under the first covenant."*

**Hebrews 9:15 (NIV)**

*"So the Christ also, having been once offered in sacrifice in order that He might bear the sins of many, will appear a second time, separated from sin, to those who are eagerly expecting Him, to make their salvation complete."*

**Hebrews 9:28 (WEY)**

2. The High Priest who entered the holy of holies typifies Jesus entering "Heaven itself" with "his own blood" on our behalf.

*"But [that appointed time came] when Christ (the Messiah) appeared as a High Priest of the better things that have come and are to come. [Then] through the greater and more perfect tabernacle not made with [human] hands, that is, not a part of this material creation, He went once for all into the [Holy of] Holies [of heaven], not by virtue of the blood of goats and calves [by which to make reconciliation between God and man], but His own blood, having found and secured a complete redemption(an everlasting release for us)."*

**Hebrews 9:11-12 (AMP)**

3. Because of Jesus' blood, it now becomes a "throne of grace" and not a throne of judgement. His blood was innocent, pure and qualified to redeem humanity.

*"Let us therefore come boldly unto the throne of grace, that we may obtain mercy, and find grace to help in time of need."*

**Hebrews 4:16**

4. His blood was substitutionary – He exchanged places with us as the scapegoat for the Israelites.

> *"Then shall he kill the goat of the sin offering, that is for the people, and bring his blood within the vail, and do with that blood as he did with the blood of the bullock, and sprinkle it upon the mercy seat, and before the mercy seat."*
>
> **Leviticus 16:15**
>
> *"Neither by the blood of goats and calves, but by his own blood he entered in once into the holy place, having obtained eternal redemption for us."*
>
> **Hebrews 9:12**

5. Though tempted in all points, yet Jesus remained without sin. This is why He was qualified to take our place.

> *"For he hath made him to be sin for us, who knew no sin; that we might be made the righteousness of God in him."*
>
> **2 Corinthians 5:21**
>
> *"For we have not an high priest which cannot be touched with the feeling of our infirmities; but was in all points tempted like as we are, yet without sin."*
>
> **Hebrews 4:15**

6. Just as the sin offerings under the Levitical priesthood were to be without blemish or defect, so was Jesus the Lamb without spot and blemish.

> *"If the priest that is anointed do sin according to the sin of the people; then let him bring for his sin, which he hath sinned, a young bullock without blemish unto the Lord for a sin offering."*
>
> **Leviticus 4:3**

**(Compare: Leviticus 4:23,28,32; 5:18; 6:6; 9:2-3; 14:10; 22:19; 23:12)**

> *"Forasmuch as ye know that ye were not redeemed with corruptible things, as silver and gold, from your vain conversation received by tradition from your fathers; But with the precious blood of Christ, as of a lamb without blemish and without spot."*
>
> **1 Peter 1:18-19**

## III. JESUS TOOK OUR PLACE

*"As many were astonished at him -- his appearance was so marred, beyond human semblance, and his form beyond that of the sons of men."*

**Isaiah 52:14 (RSV)**

*"He was despised and rejected by men; a man of sorrows, and acquainted with grief; and as one from whom men hide their faces he was despised, and we esteemed him not. Surely he has borne our griefs and carried our sorrows; yet we esteemed him stricken, smitten by God, and afflicted. But he was wounded for our transgressions, he was bruised for our iniquities; upon him was the chastisement that made us whole, and with his stripes we are healed."*

**Isaiah 53:3-5 (RSV)**

1. Keywords of **Isaiah chapters 52 and 53**

A. **Marred** – The Hebrew word is "*moshchath.*" It means disfigured.

> **Note**: Because of the beatings which Jesus took from the Roman soldiers, his outward appearance and shape was horrific to look at.

B. **Form more than sons of men** - literally says, "*His appearance was not that of a son of man...i.e., not human.*" **(Isaiah 52:14)** – This is due to the terrible beatings.

C. **Sorrows** – The Hebrew word is: "*makob.*" It means pain.

D. **Grief** – The Hebrew word is: "*choliy.*" It means sickness and disease.

> **Note**: **Matt 8:16,17** definitely states that Jesus healed all diseases on the basis of the Atonement. The Atonement was His reason for making no exceptions while healing the sick.

E. **Borne** – The Hebrew word is: "*nasa.*" It means to lift up; to carry away; to remove to a distance.

> **Note**: This is a Levitical word and applies to the scapegoat that bore the sins of the people away into the wilderness, under the old covenant. The scapegoat was a type and shadow of Jesus who would come one day and bare our sins in his own body.

> *"And the goat shall bear upon him all their iniquities unto a land not inhabited: and he shall let go the goat in the wilderness."*
>
> **Leviticus 16:22**

F. **Carried** – The Hebrew word is: "*sabal.*" It means to carry, to bear, to bear a load, to be a burden.

> **Note**: In *vs. 4,11,12*, both words "sabal" and "nasa" indicate the actual substitution and complete removal of the thing.

G. **Wounded** – The Hebrew word is: "*chalal.*" It means to pierce.

> **Note**: This refers to the piercing of his hands, feet and side.

> *"For dogs have compassed me: the assembly of the wicked have inclosed me: they pierced my hands and my feet."*
>
> **Psalm 22:16**
>
> *"But one of the soldiers with a spear pierced his side, and forthwith came there out blood and water."*
>
> **John 19:34**

H. **Bruised** – The Hebrew word is: "*daka.*" It means to smite; to beat, crush, destroy or to bruise.

> **Note**: This refers to the stripes, which the Roman soldiers put on Jesus by scourging him; the crown of thorns, and other bodily sufferings such as punching.

I. **Stripes** – The Hebrew word is: "*chabbuwrah.*" It means a black and blue mark.

2. The bible says that Jesus was, "*Smitten of God.*" (Isaiah 53:4) What does this mean?

A. It wasn't God that laid the stripes on Jesus' back, it was the Roman soldiers.

> **EX:** If somebody came in and took you outside and whipped you, that wouldn't be God who did it, it would be the person who took you and did it.

B. It wasn't God who nailed Him to the cross, it was the soldiers.

C. Verse 4 is talking about the man on the inside - Jesus' spirit. It was all laid on his spirit.

D. Jesus was never sick anymore than he sinned but yet the bible says that both our sickness and sin were laid on Him.

> *"Surely he hath borne our griefs, and carried our sorrows: yet we did esteem him stricken, smitten of God, and afflicted. But he was wounded for our transgressions, he was bruised for our iniquities: the chastisement of our peace was upon him; and with his stripes we are healed. All we like sheep have gone astray; we have turned every one to his own way; and the Lord hath laid on him the iniquity of us all."*
>
> **Isaiah 53:4-6**

E. Sickness and disease is a spiritual thing but yet it's manifested in our physical bodies.

3. What happened on the outside of Jesus' body by the soldiers is just a type of what happened on the inside.

A. If you would have been there 2000 years ago, you could have seen Jesus and watched as the Roman soldiers beat His back, but you couldn't see what was happening to the man on the inside. Our sicknesses and diseases were being laid on Him.

B. If you would have been there 2000 years ago, you could have watched as He was being nailed to the cross, but you couldn't see Him being made sin - and yet the bible says that our sins were being laid on Him. **(Isaiah 53:6)**

C. We were the ones who should have been stricken and smitten and went to hell, but instead Jesus took our place.

> *"For he hath made him to be sin for us, who knew no sin; that we might be made the righteousness of God in him."*
>
> **2 Corinthians 5:21**

D. This prophecy states that Jesus died for OUR sicknesses and OUR pains; for OUR transgressions; OUR iniquities; OUR peace and for OUR healing.

4. It's not according to God's will whether you are made whole or not, it's according to your will. He's already done something about it.

> *"Who his own self bare our sins in his own body on the tree, that we, being dead to sins, should live unto righteousness: by whose stripes ye were healed."*
>
> **1 Peter 2:24**

A. Because of not knowing it to be a redemptive right and privilege for all, most Christians when seeking to be healed by God often add to their prayers the phrase, **"If it be thy will."** Remember that faith begins when the will of God is known. Therefore how can you truly be expecting healing in your body if you do not know what the will of God is for your own life.

B. Healing of the leper - He was uncertain of God's will for him.

> *"And it came to pass, when he was in a certain city, behold a man full of leprosy: who seeing Jesus fell on his face, and besought him, saying, Lord, if thou wilt, thou canst make me clean. And he put forth his hand, and touched him, saying, I will: be thou clean. And immediately the leprosy departed from him."*
>
> **Luke 5:12,13**

> **Note**: This is the only example in the New Testament when someone actually questions the will of God concerning healing. Notice that the first thing Jesus did was to correct his theology. Jesus said unto the leper, "*I will: be thou clean.*" Jesus' message is still the same today – "*I will: be thou clean.*"

C. Healing at the pool of Bethesda

> *"After this there was a feast of the Jews; and Jesus went up to Jerusalem. Now there is at Jerusalem by the sheep market a pool, which is called in the Hebrew tongue Bethesda, having five porches. In these lay a great multitude of impotent folk, of blind, halt, withered, waiting for the moving of the water. For an angel went down at a certain season into the pool, and troubled the water: whosoever then first after the troubling of the water stepped in was made whole of whatsoever disease he had. And a certain man was there, which had an infirmity thirty and eight years. When Jesus saw him lie, and knew that he had been now a long time in that case, he saith unto him, Wilt thou be made whole? The impotent man answered him, Sir, I have no man, when the water is troubled, to put me into the pool: but while I am coming, another steppeth down before me. Jesus saith unto him, Rise, take up thy bed, and walk. And immediately the man was made whole, and took up his bed, and walked: and on the same day was the sabbath."*
>
> **John 5:1-8**

**Note**: The bible says, *"When Jesus saw him lie, and knew that he had been now a long time in that case, he saith unto him, Wilt thou be made whole?"* Have you ever wondered why would Jesus ask this question to a sick man? The answer is simple: God will not violate your will. Some people enjoy their sickness and sufferings. If they were healed, they would not have too much else to talk about and nobody to wait on them hand and foot. I've had people in the prayer line tell me that if God healed all of their problems then they would loose their disability check each month, so in the end they only wanted prayer for the major problems; they were happy to live with the minor afflictions just as long as they didn't loose their money.

D. Healing of the Syrophenician's daughter

*"Then Jesus went thence, and departed into the coasts of Tyre and Sidon. And, behold, a woman of Canaan came out of the same coasts, and cried unto him, saying, Have mercy on me, O Lord, thou Son of David; my daughter is grievously vexed with a devil. But he answered her not a word. And his disciples came and besought him, saying, Send her away; for she crieth after us. But he answered and said, I am not sent but unto the lost sheep of the house of Israel. Then came she and worshipped him, saying, Lord, help me. But he answered and said, It is not meet to take the children's bread, and to cast it to dogs. And she said, Truth, Lord: yet the dogs eat of the crumbs which fall from their masters 'table. Then Jesus answered and said unto her, O woman, great is thy faith: be it unto thee even as thou wilt. And her daughter was made whole from that very hour."*

**Matthew 15:21-28**

## IV. CONCLUSION

1. The suffering and death of Christ guarantees us that it's the will of God to heal the bodies of men and women today. Anything less would not be His best.
2. What Jesus bore in our place, we do not have to bare. He already paid the price for us.
3. When we realize the love that Christ has for every one of us, and the length He went to ensuring that sickness and disease could no longer keep us in bondage, we will no longer accept sickness and disease as "part of life," - the "hand that we've been dealt."

**- Selah -**

# LESSON 6

# REDEEMED FROM THE CURSE

## I. THE PLAN OF REDEMPTION

1. Plan of redemption - was the plan of God to rescue us from the bondage of sin and satan. Sin and satan are synonymous – He's the author of sin.

> *"He that committeth sin is of the devil; for the devil sinneth from the beginning. For this purpose the Son of God was manifested, that he might destroy the works of the devil."*
>
> **1 John 3:8**
>
> *"For sin shall not [any longer] exert dominion over you, since now you are not under Law [as slaves], but under grace [as subjects of Gods favor and mercy]."*
>
> **Romans 6:14 (AMP)**

2. When freedom from sin is granted, then you have the ability to walk free from sickness and disease.

> *"A few days later, when Jesus again entered Capernaum, the people heard that he had come home. So many gathered that there was no room left, not even outside the door, and he preached the word to them. Some men came, bringing to him a paralytic, carried by four of them. Since they could not get him to Jesus because of the crowd, they made an opening in the roof above Jesus and, after digging through it, lowered the mat the paralyzed man was lying on. When Jesus saw their faith, he said to the paralytic, Son, your sins are forgiven. Now some teachers of the law were sitting there, thinking to themselves, Why does this fellow talk like that? He's blaspheming! Who can forgive sins but God alone? Immediately Jesus knew in his spirit that this was what they were thinking in their hearts, and he said to them, Why are you thinking these things? Which is easier: to say to the paralytic, Your sins are forgiven, or to*

> *say, Get up, take your mat and walk? But that you may know that the Son of Man has authority on earth to forgive sins.... He said to the paralytic, I tell you, get up, take your mat and go home. He got up, took his mat and walked out in full view of them all. This amazed everyone and they praised God, saying, We have never seen anything like this!"*
>
> **Mark 2:1-12 (NIV)**

3. In Luke chapter 9:56, Jesus made a very definite statement. He said, "*For the Son of man is not come to destroy men's lives, but to save them.*"

   A. **Destroy** – The Greek word used here is the word, "*apollymi.*" It is the same word as used in **John 10:10.** It means to abolish, to put an end to or to render useless.

   > *"The thief cometh not, but for to steal, and to kill, and to destroy: I am come that they might have life, and that they might have it more abundantly."*
   >
   > **John 10:10**

   B. **Save** – The Greek word used here in Luke 9:56 is the word, "*sozo.*" It means to save, to heal; preserve; make whole; to rescue from danger or destruction and soundness.

   C. Jesus has come to destroy the works of the devil.

   > *"For this purpose the Son of God was manifested, that he might destroy the works of the devil."*
   >
   > **1 John 3:8**

   (1) **Destroy** – The Greek word used in this instance is the word, "*lyo.*" It means to be loosened, to release, to undo, to set free, and to do away with.

   (2) How did Jesus release us from the works of satan, such as sickness or disease?

   a. He destroyed the works of the devil and his works were sin.
   b. When freedom from sin is granted, then freedom from sickness is granted.
   c. Freedom from sickness and disease comes from knowing the truth and then acting on it.

   > *"And ye shall know the truth, and the truth shall make you free."*
   >
   > **John 8:32**

## II. CHRIST HAS REDEEMED US FROM THE CURSE OF THE LAW

> *"Christ hath redeemed us from the curse of the law, being made a curse for us: for it is written, Cursed is every one that hangeth on a tree."*
>
> **Galatians 3:13**

1. Sin always requires a penalty.

> *"For the wages which sin pays is death, but the [bountiful] free gift of God is eternal life through (in union with) Jesus Christ our Lord."*
>
> **Romans 6:23 (AMP)**
>
> *"[In fact] under the Law almost everything is purified by means of blood, and without the shedding of blood there is neither release from sin and its guilt nor the remission of the due and merited punishment for sins."*
>
> **Hebrews 9:22 (AMP)**

2. The penalty for violating the law of God was poverty, sickness, and death.

> *"However, if you do not obey the Lord your God and do not carefully follow all his commands and decrees I am giving you today, all these curses will come upon you and overtake you: You will be cursed in the city and cursed in the country. Your basket and your kneading trough will be cursed. The fruit of your womb will be cursed, and the crops of your land, and the calves of your herds and the lambs of your flocks. You will be cursed when you come in and cursed when you go out. The Lord will send on you curses, confusion and rebuke in everything you put your hand to, until you are destroyed and come to sudden ruin because of the evil you have done in forsaking him. The Lord will plague you with diseases until he has destroyed you from the land you are entering to possess. The Lord will strike you with wasting disease, with fever and inflammation, with scorching heat and drought, with blight and mildew, which will plague you until you perish...The Lord will afflict you with the boils of Egypt and with tumors, festering sores and the itch, from which you cannot be cured. The Lord will afflict you with madness, blindness and confusion of mind. At midday you will grope about like a blind man in the dark. You will be unsuccessful in everything you do; day after day you will be oppressed and robbed, with no one to rescue you...The Lord will afflict your knees and legs with painful boils that cannot be cured, spreading from the soles of your feet to the top of your head... If you do not carefully follow all the words of this law, which are written in this book, and do not revere this*

> *glorious and awesome name –the Lord your God– the Lord will send fearful plagues on you and your descendants, harsh and prolonged disasters, and severe and lingering illnesses. He will bring upon you all the diseases of Egypt that you dreaded, and they will cling to you. The Lord will also bring on you every kind of sickness and disaster not recorded in this Book of the Law, until you are destroyed."*
>
> **Deuteronomy 28:15-22, 27-29, 35,58-61(NIV)**

3. When God's people broke His commandments, they were out from His divine protection, and all He could do was to permit or allow the devil to bring these afflictions upon them. In the Hebrew language, there is a *causative* and a *permissive* tense. It's not that God caused His people to be sick, but rather He permitted or allowed them to due to their choice in violation of the covenant.

4. The death, burial, and resurrection of Jesus was God's way of releasing you and me from sin, sickness and disease.

   A. Jesus was the Lamb of God - our substitute.

> *"The next day John seeth Jesus coming unto him, and saith, Behold the Lamb of God, which taketh away the sin of the world."*
>
> **John 1:29**
>
> *"And ye know that he was manifested to take away our sins; and in him is no sin."*
>
> **1 John 3:5**

   B. The penalty that we were due, fell upon him.

> *"For the wages of sin is death, but the gift of God is eternal life in Christ Jesus our Lord."*
>
> **Romans 6:23 (NIV)**
>
> *"Going a little farther, he fell with his face to the ground and prayed, My Father, if it is possible, may this cup be taken from me. Yet not as I will, but as you will."*
>
> **Matthew 26:39 (NIV)**

   (1) On the cross God actually dealt with Jesus just as He would have treated any guilty sinner.

(2) On the cross Jesus suffered everything that we would have to suffer if we died without Christ and spent eternity in hell.

> *"About the ninth hour Jesus cried out in a loud voice, Eloi, Eloi, lama sabachthani? –which means, My God, my God, why have you forsaken me?"*
>
> **Matthew 27:46 (NIV)**

C. Jesus was not a sinner, but He bore your sins i.e., He answered to God for them.

> *"For he hath made him to be sin for us, who knew no sin; that we might be made the righteousness of God in him."*
>
> **2 Corinthians 5:21**
>
> *"For Christ is not entered into the holy places made with hands, which are the figures of the true; but into heaven itself, now to appear in the presence of God for us."*
>
> **Hebrews 9:24**

(1) He paid in full what sinners had owed.

(2) As a believer we will never have to face God in judgment for sin...i.e., God will never deal with you again as a sinner, but as a son.

> *"It was God [personally present] in Christ, reconciling and restoring the world to favor with Himself, not counting up and holding against [men] their trespasses [but cancelling them], and committing to us the message of reconciliation (of the restoration to favor)."*
>
> **2 Corinthians 5:19 (AMP)**

D. We have been made free and released from the penalty of the Law through the body of Jesus because He was our substitute.

> *"For I through the law am dead to the law, that I might live unto God."*
>
> **Galatians 2:19**
>
> *"Wherefore, my brethren, ye also are become dead to the law by the body of Christ; that ye should be married to another, even to him who is raised from the dead, that we should bring forth fruit unto God. For when we were in the flesh, the motions of sins, which were by the law did work in our members to bring forth fruit unto death. But now we are delivered from the*

> *law, that being dead wherein we were held; that we should serve in newness of spirit, and not in the oldness of the letter."*
>
> **Romans 7:4-6**

E. Jesus was not raised from the dead until we were justified i.e., made right with God.

> *"Who was delivered on account of our offences, and was raised again on account of our justification."*
>
> **Romans 4:25**

F. Through the atonement, poverty and spiritual death were removed. Since sickness and disease were one of the major effects of the curse of the law, then certainly it too has been done away with and removed.

## III. CHRIST IS SEEN IN THE VARIOUS TYPES AND SHADOWS OF THE OLD TESTAMENT

1. In the old testament, God instructed the Israelites to eat the flesh of the Passover Lamb for physical strength. Likewise when we receive Jesus into our lives, we too receive physical strength for He is the strength of our lives. The scriptures tell us that Jesus was our Passover Lamb, sacrificed for us.

> *"And they shall take of the blood, and strike it on the two side posts and on the upper door post of the houses, wherein they shall eat it. And they shall eat the flesh in that night, roast with fire, and unleavened bread; and with bitter herbs they shall eat it."*
>
> **Exodus 12:7,8**
>
> *"Purge out therefore the old leaven, that ye may be a new lump, as ye are unleavened. For even Christ our Passover is sacrificed for us."*
>
> **1 Corinthians 5:7**
>
> *"For I have received of the Lord that which also I delivered unto you, That the Lord Jesus the same night in which he was betrayed took bread: And when he had given thanks, he brake it, and said, Take, eat: this is my body, which is broken for you: this do in remembrance of me."*
>
> **1 Corinthians 11:23,24**

2. In **Leviticus 14:18,** the priest was instructed of how to make an atonement for the

leper's healing. Remember now, this is under the old covenant. If the leper could be healed because of the atonement using the blood of a sacrificial animal, then healing certainly belongs to us because of the atonement of Christ's blood.

> *"And the remnant of the oil that is in the priest's hand he shall pour upon the head of him that is to be cleansed: and the priest shall make an atonement for him before the Lord."*
>
> **Leviticus 14:18**
>
> *"He personally bore our sins in His [own] body on the tree [as on an altar and offered Himself on it], that we might die (cease to exist) to sin and live to righteousness. By His wounds you have been healed."*
>
> **1 Peter 2:24 (AMP)**

3. <u>The Brazen Serpent</u>

> *"They traveled from Mount Hor along the route to the Red Sea, to go around Edom. But the people grew impatient on the way; they spoke against God and against Moses, and said, Why have you brought us up out of Egypt to die in the desert? There is no bread! There is no water! And we detest this miserable food! Then the Lord sent venomous snakes among them; they bit the people and many Israelites died. The people came to Moses and said, We sinned when we spoke against the Lord and against you. Pray that the Lord will take the snakes away from us. So Moses prayed for the people. The Lord said to Moses, Make a snake and put it up on a pole; anyone who is bitten can look at it and live. So Moses made a bronze snake and put it up on a pole. Then when anyone was bitten by a snake and looked at the bronze snake, he lived."*
>
> **Numbers 21:4-9 (NIV)**

A. Notice that *anyone* who looked at the brazen serpent that was lifted up in the desert was healed. No one was excluded. The promise was for whosoever will.

B. As we can see from this scripture, all that was required for these dying Israelites to live was to look at the serpent of brass on the pole - the serpent symbolizing sin and brass symbolizing judgment. This was a type and shadow of Jesus who later on would come and be lifted up on the cross and judged for our sin.

> *"And just as Moses lifted up the serpent in the desert [on a pole], so must [so it is necessary that] the Son of Man be lifted up [on the cross], In order that everyone who believes in Him [who cleaves to Him, trusts*

> *Him, and relies on Him] may not perish, but have eternal life and [actually] live forever!"*
>
> **John 3:14,15 (AMP)**

C. When you keep everything in perspective in light of these verses, what you end up with is this: As the Israelites' curse was removed by the lifting up of the bronze serpent – a "type" of Christ, - our curse was certainly removed when Jesus was lifted up and nailed to the cross on account of us and made sin with our sin.

> *"Who was betrayed and put to death because of our misdeeds and was raised to secure our justification (our acquittal), [making our account balance and absolving us from all guilt before God."*
>
> **Romans 4:25 (AMP)**
>
> *"Christ hath redeemed us from the curse of the law, being made a curse <u>for us</u>: for it is written, Cursed is every one that hangeth on a tree."*
>
> **Galatians 3:13**
>
> *"Having canceled the written code, with its regulations, that was against us and that stood opposed to us; he took it away, nailing it to the cross."*
>
> **Colossians 2:14 (NIV)**
>
> *"God made him who had no sin to be sin for us, so that in him we might become the righteousness of God."*
>
> **2 Corinthians 5:21 (NIV)**

D. The only thing the Israelites had to do in order to be healed was to look at the serpent on the pole, nothing else. There was no sacrifice involved, prayer, offerings or even fasting. It was plain and simple, nothing else was expected. The same holds true under the new covenant. All we need to do is to look to Jesus as our healer. He never turns faith away empty handed!

> *"<u>Looking unto Jesus</u> the author and finisher of our faith; who for the joy that was set before him endured the cross, despising the shame, and is set down at the right hand of the throne of God."*
>
> **Hebrews 12:2**
>
> *"Jesus said unto him, If thou canst believe, all things are possible to him that believeth."*
>
> **Mark 9:23**

E. Sin is like a disease – a blood disease – that flows in the veins of every human being. There is no escaping it; it's part of the fallen nature of man. The scripture declares in Romans 3:23, *"For all have sinned, and come short of the glory of God."* Humanity continues to keep the same pattern without even looking back. People have sinned against God under the Old Testament and people sin against God under the New Testament. And you know what? The results are equally the same. Just as the deadly snakebite resulted in death back then, sin results in death today.

> *"For the wages of sin is death; but the gift of God is eternal life through Jesus Christ our Lord."*
>
> **Romans 6:23**

F. God made provision that was available to everyone who had been bitten back then. God has also made provision for those of us today that have been bitten with sickness and disease. His name is Jesus!

> *"For God so loved the world, that he gave his only begotten Son, that whosoever believeth in him should not perish, but have everlasting life."*
>
> **John 3:16**

G. When the Israelites were cured, not only were they forgiven for their sins, but they were healed in their bodies. To all who are in Christ, let us not forget all his benefits. We too are forgiven as well as healed!

> *"Bless the LORD, O my soul, and forget not all his benefits. Who forgiveth all thine iniquities; who healeth all thy diseases."*
>
> **Psalm 103:2-3**

H. Nowadays, people have a tendency to look to the preacher for the miracle they need. "If I could just get into Rev. so-and-so's prayer line and have them lay hands on me I would be healed." The mistake is that we're looking in the wrong direction. Don't get me wrong, the laying on of hands is a doctrine of the church and it has its rightful place. Nonetheless who were the Israelites instructed to look to? To their fearless leader Moses or to the serpent on the pole? Then to whom should we be looking unto if we want to see results? His name is Jesus!

> *"But seek ye first the kingdom of God, and his righteousness; and all these things shall be added unto you."*
>
> **Matthew 6:33**

> *"Looking unto Jesus the author and finisher of our faith; who for the joy that was set before him endured the cross, despising the shame, and is set down at the right hand of the throne of God."*
>
> **Hebrews 12:2**
>
> *"My message and my preaching were not with wise and persuasive words, but with a demonstration of the Spirits power, so that your faith might not rest on men's wisdom, but on Gods power."*
>
> **1 Corinthians 2:4,5 (NIV)**

4. God's **covenant of healing** with Israel.

   A. The Israelites' were guaranteed to live long healthy lives as long as they met certain conditions.

> *"And ye shall serve the LORD your God, and he shall bless thy bread thy water; and I will take sickness away from the midst of thee. There shall nothing cast their young, nor be barren, in thy land: the number of thy days I will fulfill."*
>
> **Exodus 23:25-26**

   B. Sickness is simply the result of sin and failure on the part of man to obey the Laws of God. It is part of the curse of the Law.

> *"But if you will not listen to me and carry out all these commands, and if you reject my decrees and abhor my laws and fail to carry out all my commands and so violate my covenant, then I will do this to you: I will bring upon you sudden terror, wasting diseases and fever that will destroy your sight and drain away your life. You will plant seed in vain, because your enemies will eat it. I will set my face against you so that you will be defeated by your enemies; those who hate you will rule over you, and you will flee even when no one is pursuing you."*
>
> **Leviticus 26:14-17 (NIV)**
>
> *"However, if you do not obey the Lord your God and do not carefully follow all his commands and decrees I am giving you today, all these curses will come upon you and overtake you."*
>
> **Deuteronomy 28:15 (NIV)**

   C. If God wanted the Israelites sick, then why would He promise to take sickness way from the midst of them?

D. We know from scripture that God promised man at least 70 years on the earth. How do you suppose He wants His creation to spend that time? Laid up in the hospital with sickness or disease? Unproductive, not able to move; dependant on others to wait on you hand and foot? Or do you suppose that God would rather you be healthy and fit for the Master's use?

> *"The days of our years are threescore years and ten; and if by reason of strength they be fourscore years."*
>
> **Psalm 90:10**

E. So God's covenant of healing with Israel is a type and shadow of what He intended for the church. Do you suppose that He would want to do more for the Israelites, who were only servants of the Lord, than He would want for the church, i.e., his very own sons and daughters redeemed by the blood of Jesus?

F. The Holy Spirit said through the Apostle Paul that the reason why many believers were weak, sick and die prematurely was due to not discerning or understanding the Lord's body that was broken for them. What we do not understand, we generally do not accept. And what we do not accept becomes something we cannot enjoy.

> *"For he that eateth and drinketh unworthily, eateth and drinketh damnation to himself, not discerning the Lord's body. For this cause many are weak and sickly among you, and many sleep."*
>
> **1 Corinthians 11:29-30**

## IV. CONCLUSION

1. Know that Jesus has redeemed you from the curse of poverty, sickness and spiritual death. In exchange He has transferred you into riches, health and life.

2. Read carefully *Deuteronomy 28* and know for certain what you've been delivered from. It's knowing the truth and acting on it that will set you free. As long as you stay in the dark, the enemy has an advantage over you. He thrives on our ignorance.

> *"My people are destroyed for lack of knowledge: because thou hast rejected knowledge, I will also reject thee."*
>
> **Hosea 4:6**

> *"And ye shall know the truth, and the truth shall make you free."*
>
> **John 8:32**

3. Jesus paid it all, so we can enjoy the life that God intended for us to have. Why would you want to settle for anything less. Did Jesus die in vain?

> *"He did not enter by means of the blood of goats and calves; but he entered the Most Holy Place once for all by his own blood, having obtained eternal redemption."*
>
> **Hebrews 9:12 (NIV)**
>
> *"Because by one sacrifice he has made perfect forever those who are being made holy."*
>
> **Hebrews 10:14 (NIV)**
>
> *"May the God of peace, who through the blood of the eternal covenant brought back from the dead our Lord Jesus, that great Shepherd of the sheep, equip you with everything good for doing his will, and may he work in us what is pleasing to him, through Jesus Christ, to whom be glory for ever and ever. Amen."*
>
> **Hebrews 13:20,21 (NIV)**

4. Stop looking at your symptoms and keep your eyes fixed and stayed on Jesus. The easiest way to do this is to stay in the word. If the enemy of your soul can keep you over in the arena of reasoning, he will win every time. But if you purpose in your heart to stay in the arena of faith, then you've already won – for He's the eternally defeated one!

**- Selah -**

# LESSON 7

# MUST CHRISTIANS SUFFER?

## I. IS GOD GLORIFIED BY OUR SICKNESS AND DISEASE AS SOME TEACH?

1. One popular religious tradition that satan has sold the church is that God is glorified when people suffer with sickness and disease – and that it's more noble or spiritual, for one to be patient in his suffering, as opposed to being healed.

   A. What's the first thing these self-righteous people do when they are sick? They run to the doctors and take medication; they'll do whatever it takes to alleviate the pain and discomfort.

   B. People who sincerely believe this lie should be asking God for a double portion of the disease if in fact God is glorified by it. After all, we do want to give Him glory don't we?

2. If sickness truly glorified God, then any attempt from our side to get well would actually be robbing God of the glory that He was supposed to be receiving by our suffering.

3. Let's be honest, even though people may sing how God is glorified by sickness and disease, no one actually believes it due to the obvious and that is: people choose health over sickness any day of the year. I've still to meet the person that actually prefers pain and suffering over comfort and good health.

4. If sickness glorifies God, then Jesus was a thief. Because under the ministry of Jesus, he went about doing good and healing all, everyone who came to him in need. That would mean that Jesus' ministry was one of rebellion rather than obedience. This is not in harmony with the Gospels.

> *"Now when the sun was setting, all they that had any sick with divers diseases brought them unto him; and he laid his hands on every one of them, and healed them."*
>
> **Luke 4:40**

> *"Jesus saith unto them, My meat is to do the will of him that sent me, and to finish his work."*
>
> **John 4:34**
>
> *"Then answered Jesus and said unto them, Verily, verily, I say unto you, The Son can do nothing of himself, but what he seeth the Father do: for what things soever he doeth, these also doeth the Son likewise."*
>
> **John 5:19**

5. If sickness glorified God, then someone should have notified the Holy Spirit because evidently He must have got His orders mixed up. Why do I say this? Because in the book of Acts, He continued doing the same works of Jesus, confirming the word of God and healing the sick through believers.

## II. WHEN IS GOD GLORIFIED? BEFORE OR AFTER OUR DELIVERANCE?

1. **Matthew 9:6-8** *"But that ye may know that the Son of man hath power on earth to forgive sins, (then saith he to the sick of the palsy) Arise, take up thy bed, and go unto thine house. And he arose and departed to his house. But when the multitudes saw it, they marvelled, and glorified God, which had given such power unto men."*

2. **Matthew 15:31** *"Insomuch that the multitude wondered, when they saw the dumb to speak, the maimed to be whole, the lame to walk, and the blind to see: and they glorified the God of Israel."*

3. **Mark 2:11,12** *"I say unto thee, Arise, and take up thy bed, and go thy way into thine house. And immediately he arose, took up the bed, and went forth before them all; insomuch that they were all amazed, and glorified God, saying, We never saw it on this fashion."*

4. **Luke 5:25,26** *"And immediately he rose up before them, and took up that whereon he lay, and departed to his own house, glorifying God. And they were all amazed, and they glorified God, and were filled with fear, saying, We have seen strange things today."*

5. **Luke 7:14-16** *"And he came and touched the bier: and they that bare him stood still. And he said, Young man, I say unto thee, Arise. And he that was dead sat up, and began to speak. And he delivered him to his mother. And there came a fear on all: and they glorified God, saying, That a great prophet is risen up among us; and, That God hath visited his people."*

6. **Luke 13:11-13** *"And, behold, there was a woman which had a spirit of infirmity eighteen years, and was bowed together, and could in no wise lift up herself. And when Jesus saw her, he called her*

*to him, and said unto her, Woman, thou art loosed from thine infirmity. And he laid his hands on her: and immediately she was made straight, and glorified God."*

7. **Luke 17:14-19** *"And when he saw them, he said unto them, Go shew yourselves unto the priests. And it came to pass, that, as they went, they were cleansed. And one of them, when he saw that he was healed, turned back, and with a loud voice glorified God, and fell down on his face at his feet, giving him thanks: and he was a Samaritan. And Jesus answering said, were there not ten cleansed? But where are the nine? There are not found that returned to give glory to God, save this stranger. And he said unto him, Arise, go thy way: thy faith hath made thee whole."*

8. **Luke 18:40-43** *"And Jesus stood, and commanded him to be brought unto him: and when he was come near, he asked him, Saying, What wilt thou that I shall do unto thee? And he said, Lord, that I may receive my sight. And Jesus said unto him, Receive thy sight: thy faith hath saved thee. And immediately he received his sight, and followed him, glorifying God: and all the people, when they saw it, gave praise unto God."*

9. **Luke 19:37-40** *"And when he was come nigh, even now at the descent of the mount of Olives, the whole multitude of the disciples began to rejoice and praise God with a loud voice for all the mighty works that they had seen; Saying, Blessed be the King that cometh in the name of the Lord: peace in heaven, and glory in the highest. And some of the Pharisees from among the multitude said unto him, Master, rebuke thy disciples. And he answered and said unto them, I tell you that, if these should hold their peace, the stones would immediately cry out."*

10. **John 9:3-4** *"Jesus answered, Neither hath this man sinned, nor his parents: but that the works of God should be made manifest in him. I must work the works of him that sent me, while it is day: the night cometh, when no man can work."*

11. **John 9:24** *"Then again called they the man that was blind, and said unto him, Give God the praise: we know that this man is a sinner."*

12. **John 11:4,40** *"When Jesus heard that, he said, This sickness is not unto death, but for the glory of God, that the Son of God might be glorified thereby...Jesus saith unto her, Said I not unto thee that, if thou wouldest believe, thou shouldest see the glory of God?"*

13. **Acts 3:7-9** *"And he took him by the right hand, and lifted him up: and immediately his feet and anklebones received strength. And he leaping up stood, and walked, and entered with them into the temple, walking, and leaping, and praising God. And all the people saw him walking and praising God."*

14. **Acts 4:21** *"So when they had further threatened them, they let them go, finding nothing how they might punish them, because of the people: for all men glorified God for that which was done."*

15. **Acts 9:33-35** *"And there he found a certain man named Aeneas, which had kept his bed eight years, and was sick of the palsy. And Peter said unto him, Aeneas, Jesus Christ maketh thee whole arise, and make thy bed. And he arose immediately. And all that dwelt at Lydda and Saron saw him, and turned to the Lord."*

16. **Acts 9:40-42** *"But Peter put them all forth, and kneeled down, and prayed; and turning him to the body said, Tabitha, arise. And she opened her eyes: and when she saw Peter, she sat up. And he gave her his hand, and lifted her up, and when he had called the saints and widows, presented her alive. And it was known throughout all Joppa; and many believed in the Lord."*

## III. DOES A CHRISTIAN HAVE TO SUFFER?

**Note**: The first thing Christians usually do when they hear the word suffer or suffering is to equate these terms with some type of sickness or disease. In light of this, what does the bible have to same in relation to this area?

1. A popular belief that the enemy has instilled into the minds of many believers is that if we are righteous, then we should expect sicknesses as a part of our life. For the scripture says in **Psalm 34:19,** *"Many are the afflictions of the righteous..."*

   A. Though it could include sickness, this is not what the word afflictions is referring to regardless of what the enemy has wanted you to believe. It actually means trials, hardships, persecutions and temptations, but never sicknesses or physical disabilities. Notice how Jesus used the word afflictions in the Gospel of Mark and why they came.

   > *"And have no root in themselves, and so endure but for a time: afterward, when affliction or persecution ariseth for the word's sake, immediately they are offended."*
   >
   > **Mark 4:17**

   B. Notice what the rest of **Psalm 34:19**, tells us: *"the Lord delivers us out of all of them."* So regardless of what type of affliction you're up against, the bottom line is that the Lord is there to deliver you every single time.

   C. Would God want us to bare what Christ has already borne in our behalf? Since Jesus already took your infirmities and carried away your diseases, it would be pretty ridiculous to believe that He now requires you to bear them. What purpose would that serve other than to glorify the devil.

D. One way that theologian's try and support their religious tradition is by quoting various "suffering" verses such as:

> *"Whom resist stedfast in the faith, knowing that the same afflictions are accomplished in your brethren that are in the world. But the God of all grace, who has called out to his eternal glory by Christ Jesus, after that you have suffered a while, make you perfect, establish, strengthen, and settle you."*
>
> **I Peter 5:9,10**

> **Note**: For starters, the word "afflictions" is the Greek word, "*pathema.*" It means suffering, hardship, misfortune, and evil. It is the same Greek word used in 1 Peter 5:1 – "*The elders which are among you I exhort, who am also an elder, and a witness of the sufferings of Christ.*" The suffering He's speaking of does not refer to sickness, but to the adversity and persecution that Christians had received on account of their faith and obedience to God. Peter addresses this in his letter by exhorting them to stay steadfast.

> *"And to him they agreed: and when they had called the apostles, and beaten them, they commanded that they should not speak in the name of Jesus, and let them go. And they departed from the presence of the council, rejoicing that they were counted worthy to suffer shame for his name."*
>
> **Acts 5:40-41**

2. Another popular belief and religious tradition of which I've heard since I was a child is that God chastises or corrects His children with sickness and disease. To support this fallacy, people often quote Hebrews 12:6, "*Whom the Lord loves he chastens.*" Let's look at this passage in context.

> *"And ye have forgotten the exhortation which speaketh unto you as unto children, My son, despise not thou the chastening of the Lord, nor faint when thou art rebuked of him. For whom the Lord loveth he chasteneth, and scourgeth every son whom he receiveth. If ye endure chastening, God dealeth with you as with sons; for what son is he whom the father chasteneth not? But if ye be without chastisement, whereof all are partakers, then are ye bastards,and not sons. Furthermore we have had fathers of our flesh, which corrected us, and we gave them reverence: shall we not much rather be in subjection unto the Father of spirits, and live? For they verily for a few days chastened us after their own pleasure; but he for our profit, that we might*

> *be partakers of his holiness. Now no chastening for the present seemeth to be joyous, but grievous: nevertheless afterward it yieldeth the peaceable fruit of righteousness unto them which are exercised thereby."*
>
> **Hebrews 12:5-11**

A. Yes the word does say that God "*chasteneth those whom He loves,*" but it does it say that He makes them sick? Certainly not! So where does this idea come from? Right from the pit of hell.

B. The Greek word used here is the word "*paideuo.*" It means to learn, to teach, to instruct, to train, or to educate.

C. Looking back at my education, I can't think of one instance when a teacher ever used sickness as a means of teaching the students. Sure there was discipline at times when needed, but never the use of sickness or disease.

D. As a parent, there are many ways to train up my child and to educate him or her properly, but I could never imagine using sickness or disease as a method of accomplishing this. That would be child abuse.

E. When our Heavenly Father chastens, instructs, disciplines and educates us, what makes us believe, or more specifically who's made us to believe that He does this by putting some sort of disease on us? Remember, our diseases were laid upon Jesus. He was cursed with our curse; made sick with our sicknesses and by His stripes we have been healed according to I Peter 2:24 God would not require that we bear what Jesus has already borne for us.

3. There are over 15 different Greek words with 15 different meanings that are all translated by one word in the English Bible suffered, suffer, or suffering."

A. Not one case does any of the suffering ever refer to a Christian suffering with sickness, disease, or poverty. For example take Matthew 19:14:

> *"But Jesus said, Suffer little children, and forbid them not, to come unto me."*
>
> **Matthew 19:14**

B. Religion would want you to believe that sickness, disease and afflictions come directly from the Father, i.e., it is His visitation to you, but this is not scripturally based. Let us not be ignorant or else the enemy will have an advantage over us.

C. Sickness and disease is not God's way of punishing you. He has only one penalty for in and that is death.

> *"For the wages of sin is death; but the gift of God is eternal life through Jesus Christ our Lord."*
>
> **Romans 6:23**

4. The more you are used of God, the greater the attacks because you have become a threat to satan - you're his enemy and he wants you out of here.

> *"We are in deep trouble for bringing you God's comfort and salvation. But in our trouble God has comforted us--and this, too, to help you: to show you from our personal experience how God will tenderly comfort you when you undergo these same sufferings. He will give you the strength to endure. I think you ought to know, dear brothers, about the hard time we went through in Asia. We were really crushed and overwhelmed, and feared we would never live through it. We felt we were doomed to die and saw how powerless we were to help ourselves; but that was good, for then we put everything into the hands of God, who alone could save us, for he can even raise the dead. And he did help us and saved us from a terrible death; yes, and we expect him to do it again and again."*
>
> **2 Corinthians 1:8-10 (Living)**

> **Note**: In 2 Corinthians 4:4, Jesus referred to Satan as *"the god of this world."* Why are we told to wear the armour of God if there isn't any enemy? We are on enemy grounds and will be attached from time to time.

5. The only suffering that a Christian should suffer is persecution.

> *"Remember the word that I said unto you, The servant is not greater than his lord. If they have persecuted me, they will also persecute you."*
>
> **John 15:20**
>
> *"Dear friends, do not be surprised at the painful trial you are suffering, as though something strange were happening to you. But rejoice that you participate in the sufferings of Christ, so that you may be overjoyed when his glory is revealed. If you are insulted because of the name of Christ, you are blessed, for the Spirit of glory and of God rests on you. If you suffer, it should not be as a murderer or thief or any other kind of criminal, or even as a meddler. However, if you suffer as a Christian, do not be ashamed, but*

> *praise God that you bear that name."*
>
> **1 Peter 4:12-16 (NIV)**

6. God doesn't decree that you're going to suffer, but you are on enemy grounds and he will try and persecute you.

> *"You, however, know all about my teaching, my way of life, my purpose, faith, patience, love, endurance, persecutions, sufferings–what kinds of things happened to me in Antioch, Iconium and Lystra, the persecutions I endured. Yet the Lord rescued me from all of them. In fact, everyone who wants to live a godly life in Christ Jesus will be persecuted."*
>
> **2 Timothy 3:10-12 (NIV)**

## IV. CONCLUSION

1. Since Jesus Christ suffered for us; in our place, as our substitute we can now enjoy the abundant life that He came to give.

> *"The thief comes only in order to steal and kill and destroy. I came that they may have and enjoy life, and have it in abundance (to the full, till it overflows)."*
>
> **John 10:10 (AMP)**

2. The only "cross" you are to carry in life, is obedience to the plan, purpose and will of God for your life. God will never ask you to carry something that He laid upon Jesus.

> *"Then Jesus said to his disciples, If anyone would come after me, he must deny himself and take up his cross and follow me. For whoever wants to save his life will lose it, but whoever loses his life for me will find it."*
>
> **Matthew 16:24,25 (NIV)**

3. Attacks will come from the enemy, but "*having done all to stand, keep standing*" on the Word of God . If God is for you, then who can be against you!

4. Remember that no weapon formed against you will prosper! (**Isaiah 54:17**)

5. If healing and deliverance glorifies God the sickness and disease glorifies the devil.

**- Selah -**

# LESSON 8

# KNOW WHO THE ENEMY IS

## I. WHO BRINGS THE TESTS AND TRIALS? RELIGION SAYS GOD DOES.

1. One of the characteristics of God is that He is omniscient, i.e., all knowing. He knows what we've gone through or are going through right now in our life. He will never abandon us, leaving us to fend for ourselves. He will always lead us in victory, overcoming every obstacle that the enemy may set before us.

> *"Now thanks be unto God, which always causeth us to triumph in Christ."*
> **2 Corinthians 2:14**

2. If you don't know who your enemy is, then you might blame God.

> *"To keep Satan from getting the advantage over us; for we are not ignorant of his wiles and intentions."*
> **2 Corinthians 2:11 (AMP)**

> *"For we wrestle not against flesh and blood, but against principalities, against powers, against the rulers of the darkness of this world, against spiritual wickedness in high places. Wherefore take unto you the whole armor of God, that ye may be able to withstand in the evil day, and having done all, to stand."*
> **Ephesians 6:12-13**

3. Satan wants to find your breaking point. You're his target. God already knows your limit.

> *"Blessed is the man that endureth temptation: for when he is tried, he shall receive the crown of life, which the Lord hath promised to them that love him. Let no man say when he is tempted, I am tempted of God: for God cannot be*

> *tempted with evil, neither tempteth he any man."*
>
> **James 1:12-13**

A. If God is not the one tempting you, then where is the temptation coming from?

B. Satan doesn't know what you're going to do. He's not omniscient so he has to test you. He really doesn't know anything except what you tell him or what he programs into your mind through thoughts.

C. For this reason we are instructed in the word of God to take every thought captive.

> *"Casting down imaginations, and every high thing that exalteth itself against the knowledge of God, and bringing into captivity every thought to the obedience of Christ."*
>
> **2 Corinthians 10:5**

4. What God does is search our hearts in the midst of the trial. He's looking for that one ingredient, which pleases him called FAITH.

> *"I the LORD search the heart, I try the reins, even to give every man according to his ways, and according to the fruit of his doings."*
>
> **Jeremiah 17:10**
>
> *"Let a man so account of us, as of the ministers of Christ, and stewards of the mysteries of God. Moreover it is required in stewards, that a man be found faithful."*
>
> **1 Corinthians 4:1-2**
>
> *"But without faith it is impossible to please him: for he that cometh to God must believe that he is, and that he is a rewarder of them that diligently seek him."*
>
> **Hebrews 11:6**

5. Satan tempts your body and soul (mind, will and emotions), but God tries and proves the heart in the midst of the trial to see how you will respond.

> **Note**: It is when adversity comes that will determine where your level of faith is.

6. What about **Genesis 22:1?** The bible says, "*God did tempt Abraham.*"

A. The Hebrews word for the word tempt is the word, "*nasa*" – It means to tempt, try or prove. All three are expressed by the same word.

B. Keep in mind though, God tempts no man, satan is the tempter. And while satan was busy tempting Abraham to disobey an instruction (i.e., to take Isaac and sacrifice him), God was proving his heart, not drawing him into sin.

C. Certainly, Abraham could have disobeyed God if he wanted to and then would have been responsible for both his actions as well as the consequences for disobedience, but thank God He obeyed.

> **Note**: There will be times in your life when temptation is knocking at your door and yes, you do have a choice. Take for example a lifeguard whose responsibility is to watch a specific designated area on the beach. Though swimmers are advised to remain within the designated swimming area, if they so choose, they can wander into some dangerous waters. If the lifeguard can't see them, then he cannot help them. Though they were permitted to wander off on their own, they were never encouraged to do so. Hence they are now responsible for both their actions as well as the consequences.

D. Doesn't God permit persecution, suffering and affliction?

1. First of all realize that permission is not the same as commission. In the Hebrew there is a causative tense and a permissive tense. At a general glance some passages may appear confusing and contrary to the nature and character of God. Without proper study of His word, you will not get the true thought or meaning behind certain passages.

2. Yes, God permits things to happen in the earth. He has certain laws that He's set in motion. When an individual comes in contact with these laws, they will work – both for the believer and unbeliever alike. But when we violate these laws, as I've pointed out earlier, we are responsible for the outcome. We cannot blame God, for something that we brought on ourselves.

## II. GOD PROVIDES THE WAY OF ESCAPE

1. Satan brings the trial, but God makes the way of escape.

> *"There hath no temptation taken you but such as is common to man: but God is faithful, who will not suffer you to be tempted above that ye are able but*

> *will with the temptation also make a way to escape, that ye may be able to bear it."*
>
> **1 Corinthians 10:13**

A. The word "able" in the Greek is the word, *"dunamai."* It means might, to be possible, to be of power, to be capable, and to be able to do something. The Strong's number is 1410.

B. In Acts 1:8, Jesus said, *"But ye shall receive power after that the Holy Ghost is come upon you."* The Greek word for power used in this instance is the word, *"dunamis."* It means might or ability; strength, power; inherent power residing in a thing. The Strong's number is 1411. So *dunamis* is the child of *dunamai.*

2. Two ways of escape that have been provided for you:

A. Through the grace of God. (*This is when God puts the apple on our tree, because our faith is not producing any fruit*).

B. Through the victory of the Lord Jesus revealed to us in the Word of God.

> *"For whatsoever is born of God overcometh the world: and this is the victory that overcometh the world, even our faith."*
>
> **1 John 5:4**

(1) Our faith is to be placed in what He did for us.
(2) Your faith is the key to your victory.

> *"Nay, in all these things we are more than conquerors through him that loved us."*
>
> **Romans 8:37**

> **EX**: Two heavyweight boxers who battle it out. The winner takes the check home to his wife who will enjoy the prize yet never did fight.

C. Here's a clue of how to get victory; how to stay in victory and how to enjoy the abundant life that Jesus came to give us.

> *"I have written unto you, fathers, because ye have known him that is from the beginning. I have written unto you, young men, because ye are*

> *strong, and the word of God abideth in you, and ye have overcome the wicked one."*
>
> **1 John 2:14**

(1) Notice why they are strong…it's because the word of God abideth in them.
(2) The spoken word of God is the sword of the spirit.

> *"And take the helmet of salvation, and the sword of the Spirit, which is the word of God."*
>
> **Ephesians 6:17**

3. God provides the way of escape but YOU have to take it. YOU will have to exercise your authority of the devil; over sickness and disease.

4. There is nothing that satan can ever bring against you that God hasn't already made the provision so you could overcome.

5. If satan is allowed into the arena with you, that's because God knows you can take him.

## III. IT'S ONLY IN THE ARENA OF LIFE THAT YOU GO THROUGH, THAT YOU DISCOVER GOD'S WORD WORKS.

> **EX:** How would you know if God will supply all your needs if you never had any?

1. The only way for you as an individual to know it as a fact in your life is for you to experience it.

2. God doesn't send trials on you for you to go under, the enemy does. God knows that through Christ you can walk over them and be more than a conqueror.

> *"I can do all things through Christ which strengtheneth me."*
>
> **Philippians 4:13**

> *"Jesus said unto him, If thou canst believe, all things are possible to him that believeth."*
>
> **Mark 9:23**

3. Look where you are sitting. (*And it shouldn't be under the circumstances.*)

*"That the God of our Lord Jesus Christ, the Father of glory, may give unto you the spirit of wisdom and revelation in the knowledge of him: The eyes of your understanding being enlightened; that ye may know what is the hope of his calling, and what the riches of the glory of his inheritance in the saints, And what is the exceeding greatness of his power to us-ward who believe, according to the working of his mighty power, Which he wrought in Christ, when he raised him from the dead, and set him at his own right hand in the heavenly places, Far above all principality, and power, and might, and dominion, and every name that is named, not only in this world, but also in that which is to come: And hath put all things under his feet, and gave him to be the head over all things to the church, Which is his body, the fullness of him that filleth all in all."*

**Ephesians 1:17-23**

*"And hath raised us up together, and made us sit together in heavenly places in Christ Jesus."*

**Ephesians 2:6**

**Note**: Since all things are under our feet, it would have to include sickness and disease or else it's not all things.

## IV. CONCLUSION

1. Know who sickness and disease comes from. John 10:10 says it's from the thief.

*"The thief comes only to steal and kill and destroy; I have come that they may have life, and have it to the full."*

**John 10:10 (NIV)**

2. By studying the Word of God you will increase your discernment. You'll be able to tell if this is God's will or from the enemy. You'll know why things are happening or not happening in your life.

*"Study to shew thyself approved unto God, a workman that needeth not to be ashamed, rightly dividing the word of truth."*

**2 Timothy 2:15**

3. Satan thrives on ignorance however when you are aware of his operations, schemes, and tactics, then you have an advantage over him.

> *"And ye shall know the truth, and the truth shall make you free."*
>
> **John 8:32**
>
> *"Lest Satan should get an advantage of us: for we are not ignorant of his devices."*
>
> **2 Corinthians 2:11**

4. Allow the Holy Spirit to enlighten you. When He does, faith will begin to rise up within your heart. You'll begin to rise exercise your authority. You'll stretch forth your hand and say, "sickness, disease, infirmity, I take authority over you! I break your hold on me! Go from me now! I cancel your assignment! I declare this battle is over and the victory is mine in Jesus name!

5. Remember, you're not the sick trying to get healed, you are the healed protecting your health in Jesus name!

**- Selah -**

# LESSON 9

# JOB'S STORY

## I. WHAT ABOUT JOB? DIDN'T GOD AFFLICT HIM AND TEST HIM AND BRING SICKNESS AND DESTRUCTION ON HIM?

> *"Now there was a day when the sons of God came to present themselves before the LORD, and Satan came also among them. And the LORD said unto Satan, Whence comest thou? Then Satan answered the LORD, and said, From going to and fro in the earth, and from walking up and down in it. And the LORD said unto Satan, Hast thou considered my servant Job, that there is none like him in the earth, a perfect and an upright man, one that feareth God, and turns away from evil? Then Satan answered the LORD, and said, Doth Job fear God for nought? Hast not thou made an hedge about him, and about his house, and about all that he hath on every side? Thou hast blessed the work of his hands, and his substance is increased in the land. But put forth thine hand now, and touch all that he hath, and he will curse thee to thy face. And the LORD said unto Satan, Behold, all that he hath is in thy power; only upon himself put not forth thine hand. So Satan went forth from the presence of the LORD."*
>
> **Job 1:6-12**

1. The hedge was already down and satan didn't even know it.

   A. Satan doesn't know everything. He only knows what you tell him or what he programs into your mind and gets you to act on. This is why we need to weigh every thought in light of God's word. If it doesn't agree, then cast it down.

> *"Casting down imaginations, and every high thing that exalteth itself against the knowledge of God, and bringing into captivity every thought to the obedience of Christ."*
>
> **2 Corinthians 10:5**

B. Some have put satan on a pedestal and placed him next to God thinking he is omnipresent, omnipotent and omniscient and he is not. He is an angel and can only be in one place at one time. He's not God. He doesn't know everything.

C. He used to be called, "the anointed cherub" meaning at one time he had an anointing on him and he knew the mind of God. But when he sinned he lost his anointing because he doesn't understand the Bible - it is spiritually discerned. He reads it just like the natural unregenerate man would and doesn't comprehend it.

2. Bible scholars agree that all these series of bad events transpired within twelve months. This did not span out over Job's entire life.

A. *"All your camels have been stolen."*

B. *"All your oxen have been stolen."*

C. *"All your fields and crops have been burnt up."*

D. *"Your children are dead."*

3. Job's heart was upright, but his mind was deceived. When you consider some of the things that came out of Job's own mouth, you have to realize that he did not always have all the right answers.

> *"There was a man in the land of Uz, whose name was Job; and that man was perfect and upright, and one that feared God, and eschewed evil."*
>
> **Job 1:1**
>
> *"The Lord gave, and the Lord hath taken away; blessed be the name of the Lord."*
>
> **Job 1:21**

A. This is not a statement of truth. Verse *12* tells us that satan did this not God. God is a good God. He is the life giver.

B. Job thought God did this so he attributed it to God. It was satan, who came and stole from him.

C. He willingly accepted it because He thought it was from God and yet still managed to keep a right heart attitude about everything that had taken place.

> **<u>Note</u>:** This is exactly what satan has been using against the Church. When you think that God is responsible for the calamity, then you won't seek any help at least not from Him. Instead, you'll accept it.

D. God doesn't give and take away.

> *"For the gifts and calling of God are without repentance."*
>
> **Romans 11:29**

> **<u>Note</u>:** A person's gift may become inoperative because of a sinful lifestyle, but they don't lose it.

E. A common question people often ask is: "Didn't God permit satan to afflict Job?" The answer is yes. Though God permits everything, we need to understand that permission is not the same as commission. God stood by and watched Adam sin in the beginning, but He remember that He did tell Adam not to do it. Adam had been given the right to choose, therefore God had to permit him to make the choice. If God's not permitting things to happen, that means there is a power greater than him.

## II. JOB BROUGHT THIS ON HIMSELF

> *"For the thing which I greatly feared is come upon me, and that which I was afraid of is come unto me."*
>
> **Job 3:25**

1. Job was a man who started out in faith, but then He stepped over into fear, doubt and unbelief. When he did, the hedge came down. Instead of trusting God and committing his children to the Lord, Job was continually making provision for their possible failures.

> *"And it was so, when the days of their feasting were gone about, that Job sent and sanctified them, and rose up early in the morning, and offered burnt offerings according to the number of them all: for Job said, <u>It may be</u> that my sons have sinned, and cursed God in their hearts. <u>Thus did Job continually</u>."*
>
> **Job 1:5**

2. Fear opens the door to satan, sickness and oppression every time. Job continually made provision for fear and in the end fear got the best of him. "*For the thing, which I greatly feared has come upon me.*" Making provision is a good thing if

it's done in faith, but making provision when motivated by fear gives place to the devil.

3. The question to ask ourselves is: What is motivating us to do what we do, say what we say and go where we go? Is it faith – based on God's word, or fear that's behind it?

> **Note**: Fear is the opposite of faith and works the same way only against you instead of for you. If you're afraid of something, it's because you believe in it. You cannot be afraid of something you do not believe exists. When a person continually thinks, speaks and imagines the worst-case scenarios, then he or she is planning for the worst.

4. Fear and faith cannot operate in the same environment. One pleases God and the other does not.

> *"But without faith it is impossible to please him: for he that cometh to God must believe that he is, and that he is a rewarder of them that diligently seek him."*
>
> **Hebrews 11:6**

5. His fear drove out his faith. He later confessed that fear is what opened the door.

6. Job admitted that he spoke without knowledge.

> *"Therefore have I uttered that I understood not; things too wonderful for me, which I knew not."*
>
> **Job 42:3 (NIV)**

## III. THE MOMENT THAT JOB REPENTED AND PRAYED FOR HIS THREE FRIENDS, HE WAS INSTANTLY DELIVERED.

> *"And the LORD turned the captivity of Job, when he prayed for his friends: also the LORD gave Job twice as much as he had before."*
>
> **Job 42:10**

1. Who was Job in captivity to? SATAN. In **Acts 10:38**, notice who the oppressor is.

> *"How God anointed Jesus of Nazareth with the Holy Ghost and with power: who went about doing good, and healing all that were oppressed of the devil; for God was with him."*

2. Who delivered him? GOD

> *"Many are the afflictions of the righteous: but the LORD delivereth him out of them all."*
>
> **Psalm 34:19**

3. God doesn't take people captive. He is the liberator and satan is the oppressor.

> *"Now the Lord is that Spirit: and where the Spirit of the Lord is, there is liberty."*
>
> **2 Corinthians 3:17**

4. After all this ordeal, Job lived a 140 years longer and saw his children and their children, to the fourth generation.

> *"After this lived Job an hundred and forty years, and saw his sons, and his sons 'sons, even four generations."*
>
> **Job 42:16**

## IV. CONCLUSION

1. Job was simply a man that missed the mark just like some of us do from time to time. When he got over into fear and unbelief, the door was opened, the hedge came down and satan started afflicting him.

2. Satan has no place in your life unless you give it to him. The apostle Paul warned the Ephesians in chapter 4:27, "*Neither give place to the devil.*"

3. Ignorance also gives satan an entrance into your life as well as sin. Don't be guilty of either one.

> *"My people are destroyed for lack of knowledge."*
>
> **Hosea 4:6**

4. We are protected if we believe and obey the Word of God. Confession is not enough. Your faith and love for God is demonstrated by your obedience. Jesus said, "*If ye love me, keep my commandments.*" (John 14:15)

**- Selah -**

# LESSON 10

# PAUL'S THORN IN THE FLESH

*"It is not expedient for me doubtless to glory. I will come to visions and revelations of the Lord. I knew a man in Christ above fourteen years ago, (whether in the body, I cannot tell; or whether out of the body, I cannot tell: God knoweth;) such an one caught up to the third heaven. And I knew such a man, (whether in the body, or out of the body, I cannot tell: God knoweth;) How that he was caught up into paradise, and heard unspeakable words, which it is not lawful for a man to utter. Of such an one will I glory: yet of myself I will not glory, but in mine infirmities. For though I would desire to glory, I shall not be a fool; for I will say the truth but now I forbear, lest any man should think of me above that which he seeth me to be, or that he heareth of me. And lest I should be exalted above measure through the abun- dance of the revelations, there was given to me a thorn in the flesh, the messenger of Satan to buffet me, lest I should be exalted above measure. For this thing I be-sought the Lord thrice, that it might depart from me. And he said unto me, My grace is sufficient for thee: for my strength is made perfect in weakness. Most gladly therefore will I rather glory in my infirmities, that the power of Christ may rest upon me. Therefore I take pleasure in infirmities, in reproaches, in necessities, in persecutions, in distresses for Christ's sake: for when I am weak, then am I strong."*

**2 Corinthians 12:1-10**

## I. INTRODUCTION

The word infirmities in the Greek is "*astheneia*." It means: weakness; an inability to perform up to standard or par. This could include anything as well as physical illness. The subject here is the "thorn in the flesh." Many people say that the thorn in the flesh was a sickness or disease. Let's find out. The Bible is a pretty fair commentary on itself. If the term "thorn in the flesh" is a sickness or disease or a physical ailment of any kind, then it is at least reasonable to believe that somewhere else in the Bible we would find some evidence, perhaps

even another case. Surely it would be mentioned somewhere. Let's examine this. Does this term, "thorn in-the-flesh" occur any where else in the Bible? If so, how does it use this term?

1. How is the term, "thorn in the flesh" used elsewhere in the bible?

> *"And the LORD spake unto Moses in the plains of Moab by Jordan near Jericho, saying, Speak unto the children of Israel, and say unto them, When ye are passed over Jordan into the land of Canaan; Then ye shall drive out all the inhabitants of the land from before you, and destroy all their pictures, and destroy all their molten images, and quite pluck down all their high places: And ye shall dispossess the inhabitants of the land, and dwell therein: for I have given you the land to possess it. And ye shall divide the land by lot for an inheritance among your families: and to the more ye shall give the more inheritance, and to the fewer ye shall give the less inheritance: every man's inheritance shall be in the place where his lot falleth; according to the tribes of your fathers ye shall inherit. But if ye will not drive out the inhabitants of the land from before you; then it shall come to pass, that those which ye let remain of them shall be pricks in your eyes, and thorns in your sides, and shall vex you in the land wherein ye dwell."*
>
> **Numbers 33:50-55**

A. Summary of **Numbers 33:50-55**

(1) "Thorn in the side" – is the same thing as "thorn in the flesh." God said the inhabitants will be this to them.
(2) Did God mean these people will be sticking out of their side?
(3) Thorns are used figuratively as people.
(4) He's saying these people would irritate you like a thorn in your flesh.
(5) It was not talking about sickness or disease but people.

> *"For the LORD hath driven out from before you great nations and strong: but as for you, no man hath been able to stand before you unto this day. One man of you shall chase a thousand: for the LORD your God, he it is that fighteth for you, as he hath promised you. Take good heed therefore unto yourselves, that ye love the LORD your God. Else if ye do in any wise go back, and cleave unto the remnant of these nations, even these that remain among you, and shall make marriages with them, and go in unto them, and they to you: Know for a certainty that the LORD your God will no more drive out any of these nations from before you; but they shall be snares and traps unto you, and scourges in your sides, and thorns in your eyes, until ye perish from off this good land which the LORD your God hath given you."*
>
> **Joshua 23:9-13**

B. Summary of **Joshua 23:9-13**

(1) "Thorns in your eyes..." - is the same thing as "thorn in the flesh."
(2) What was he talking about? People, not sickness or disease.
(3) We can see he was using them figuratively.

> *"And an angel of the LORD came up from Gilgal to Bochim, and said, I made you to go up out of Egypt, and have brought you unto the land which I sware unto your fathers; and I said, I will never break my covenant with you. And ye shall make no league with the inhabitants of this land; ye shall throw..."down their altars: but ye have not obeyed my voice: why have ye done this? therefore I also said, I will not drive them out from before you; but they shall be as thorns in your sides, and their gods shall be a snare unto you. And it came to pass, when the angel of the LORD spake these words unto all the children of Israel, that the people lifted up their voice, and wept."*
>
> **Judges 2:1-4**

C. Summary of **Judges 2:1-4**

(1) "Thorns in your sides…" are used here as a figure of speech.
(2) **EX**: "So and so is a pain in the neck." Do you mean that the person actually was in your neck? No.

> *"Although my house be not so with God; yet he hath made with me an everlasting covenant, ordered in all things, and sure: for this is all my salvation, and all my desire, although he make it not to grow. But the sons of Belial shall be all of them as thorns thrust away, because they cannot be taken with hands."*
>
> **2 Samuel 23:6**

D. Summary of **2 Samuel 23:5-6**

(1) Notice the "sons of Belial shall be as thorns."
(2) No reference here of any kind of sickness or disease.

2. In every case thorn is used figuratively and always was talking about personalities.

> *"There was given to me a thorn in the flesh, the messenger of Satan."*
>
> **2 Corinthians 12:7**

3. "Thorn in the flesh" is merely a figure of speech; an idiom every single time.

4. What context did Jesus use thorns?

> *"And these are they which are sown among thorns; such as hear the word, And the cares of this world, and the deceitfulness of riches, and the lusts of other things entering in, choke the word, and it becometh unfruitful."*
>
> **Mark 4:18,19**

> **Note**: The purpose for Paul's thorn in the flesh was to choke the word of God that He had received.

5. Paul tells you exactly what the thorn was, "the messenger of satan." He should know what it was because he was the one with the problem.

6. Who was this messenger of satan?

   A. The Greek word for **messenger** is "*angelos*." It appears 186 times in the New Testament. 179 times it is translated as "angels" and 7 times it is translated as the word "messenger."

   B. Not one time is "*angelos*" used to describe a thing such as sickness or disease but it **always** refers to a personality.

   C. Seven times out of seven this word refers to a messenger.

> **Matthew 11:10** – *"For this is he, of whom it is written, Behold, I send my messenger before thy face, which shall prepare thy way before thee."*
>
> **Mark 1:2** – *"As it is written in the prophets, Behold, I send my messenger before thy face, which shall prepare thy way before thee."*
>
> **Luke 7:24** – *"And when the messengers of John were departed, he began to speak unto the people concerning John, What went ye out into the wilderness for to see? A reed shaken with the wind?"*
>
> **Luke 7:27** – *"This is he, of whom it is written, Behold, I send my messenger before thy face, which shall prepare thy way before thee."*
>
> **Luke 9:52** – *"And sent messengers before his face: and they went, and entered into a village of the Samaritans, to make ready for him."*
>
> **2 Corinthians 12:7** – *"And lest I should be exalted above measure through*

> *the abundance of the revelations, there was given to me a thorn in the flesh, the messenger of Satan to buffet me."*
>
> **James 2:25** – *"Likewise also was not Rahab the harlot justified by works, when she had received the messengers, and had sent them out another way?"*

D. Satan assigned one of his angels to Paul to stop him because if Paul got out he would cause a lot of trouble for satan.

E. Paul tells you it wasn't from God but from satan.

F. What was the messenger there for?

(1) Paul tells you it was given to buffet him.
(2) The Greek word for **buffet** is the word, "*kolaphizo*." It means to strike blow after blow; to strike repeatedly; to contend against; to oppose; constant repeated attacks.
(3) Not one time is the word buffet used to describe sickness and disease.

> **Matthew 26:67** – *"Then did they spit in his face, and buffeted him; and others smote him with the palms of their hands."*
>
> **Mark 14:65** – *"And some began to spit on him, and to cover his face, and to buffet him, and to say unto him, Prophesy: and the servants did strike him with the palms of their hands."*
>
> **1 Corinthians 4:11** – *"Even unto this present hour we both hunger, and thirst, and are naked, and are buffeted, and have no certain dwelling place."*
>
> **1 Peter 2:20** – *"For what glory is it, if, when ye be buffeted for your faults, ye shall take it patiently? but if, when ye do well, and suffer for it, ye take it patiently, this is acceptable with God."*

(4) It was given or assigned to Paul so he couldn't be "*exalted above measure.*"

> **Note**: This wasn't given to Paul just so he wouldn't exalt Himself. This scripture is not talking about self-exaltation. The word **exalt** means: to elevate, to lift up or to raise. **Above measure** means: to throw beyond the usual mark. God's revelation lifts us, throws us up beyond the normal way of thinking. By walking in the promises of God, in His divine revelations, you

> are lifted up; raised up and thrown beyond the usual mark of living. No longer are we captivated by sickness, but now walk in health. No longer does satan lord and have dominion over us but we exercise authority over him. As we get into the word of God and His word gets into us, we begin to discover who we are in Christ, what we have in Christ and what we can do in Christ.

(5) The author of revelations is God.

> *"That the God of our Lord Jesus Christ, the Father of glory, may give unto you the spirit of wisdom and revelation in the know-ledge of him."*
>
> **Ephesians 1:17**

(6) Satan came to annoy Paul and tried to prevent him from walking in the abundance of revelation knowledge that God had given to him. As Paul walked in this revelation, he would be able to teach others so they too might walk in the light.

(7) If the thorn was a sickness or disease, then in order to fulfill the word "buffet" that would mean Paul would have been sick all his life.

7. If Paul was sick and could do all he did and write half the New Testament, it sure didn't stop him from doing his job now did it?

> **EX:** For some people, even a runny nose shuts down their schedule for days. "I'm feeling like I'm coming down with the flu. I'll have to stay home from work."

8. Paul chose to lay his life down and die a martyr. He knew he finished his course. He didn't have to have his head cut-off.

> **Note**: Think of all the Christians who have died of disease and never finished their course. If we're going to imitate Paul, then we're going to have to be victorious, because nothing stopped Paul from getting the job done. So you can't use Paul as an excuse for being sick.

## II. HOW MUCH TROUBLE DID THIS MESSENGER CAUSE PAUL?

1. **Acts 9:23-25** - Jews took council to kill him right after his conversion.

2. **Acts 9:26-29** - He was hindered in joining the Christians.

3. **Acts 13:44-49** - He was opposed by Jews in a mob.

4. **Acts 13:50-52** - He was expelled out of Antioch.

5. **Acts 14:1-5** - He was mobbed and expelled out of Iconium.

6. **Acts 14:6-19** - Stoned and left for dead.

7. **Acts 16:12-40** - He was beaten and jailed at Philippi.

8. **Acts 17:1-10** - He was mobbed and expelled from Thessonalica.

9. **Acts 17:10-14** - He was mobbed and expelled from Beria.

10. **Acts 18:1-23** - He was mobbed at Corinth.

11. **Acts 19:8** - He was continually disputing with false brethren.

12. **Acts 19:23-31** - He was mobbed at Ephesus.

13. **Acts 20:3** - There was a plot against his life by the Jews.

14. **2 Corinthians 11:23-27** - Further persecution.

## III. MY GRACE IS SUFFICIENT

1. What grace is He talking about?

   A. Everything that Jesus has bought and paid for in His death, burial and resurrection.

   B. Satan's defeat was your victory.

> *"Nay, in all these things we are more than conquerors through him that loved us."*
>
> **Romans 8:37**

> *"But thanks be to God, which giveth us the victory through our Lord Jesus Christ."*
>
> **1 Corinthians 15:57**
>
> *"Now thanks be unto God, which always causeth us to triumph in Christ."*
>
> **2 Corinthians 2:14**

C. The authority of the believer has been restored. That's the grace He's talking about.

> *"And Jesus came and spake unto them, saying, All power is given unto me in heaven and in earth. Go ye therefore, and teach all nations, baptizing them in the name of the Father, and of the Son, and of the Holy Ghost."*
>
> **Matthew 28:18,19**
>
> *"And these signs shall follow them that believe; In my name shall they cast out devils."*
>
> **Mark 16:17**

D. What are we to do with this authority? We are to use the name of Jesus and get satan off our own back. If we couldn't do this then why does the bible tell us to resist him?

> *"So be subject to God. Resist the devil [stand firm against him], and he will flee from you."*
>
> **James 4:7 (AMP)**
>
> *"Be sober, be vigilant; because your adversary the devil, as a roaring lion, walketh about, seeking whom he may devour: Whom resist stedfast in the faith."*
>
> **1 Peter 5:8,9**

E. God has done everything He's going to do. Now it's up to us to enforce satan's defeat. We have the means to do so: the name of Jesus, the word of God and the Holy Ghost.

2. Why did He pray three times?

A. First, we need to understand that the Bible is progressive Revelation.

> **EX:** Abraham knew more than Adam; Moses knew more than Abraham; Paul knew more than Moses.

> <u>**Note**</u> Paul didn't sit down at one time and write all his letters. This took place over a period of years. We have the advantage over Paul because we can look at the whole scope of revelation at one time.

B. Second, we need to understand that Paul learned he learned over a period of time. At this particular period, apparently Paul didn't understand the full meaning of the power in the Name of Jesus. If he did he could have used it.

C. Third, we need to understand that the Gospels weren't written so he didn't have the advantage of going and reading **Mark 16:17** or **James 4:7**.

3. What did the Lord mean, by "*my strength is made perfect in weakness?*" (**vs 9**)

A. <u>Firstly,</u> you have to understand that man relative to God is weak; helpless. Man was made to be dependent upon God. Jesus said in John 15 5, "*For without me ye can do nothing.*" When we are weak, then He is strong.

B. <u>Secondly</u>, we have to realize that God's glory and power is manifested in weak, fragile earthly vessels. As amazing as the human body is, it can be destroyed.

C. I believe what the Lord was saying to Paul is that He's wanting to manifest his presence in us and through us. For when a man or woman is anointed by God, then can he or she turn the world upside down and do exploits. God gets the glory out of it because everybody knows that it wasn't the vessel, but the treasure in the vessel. We are to be "strong in the Lord and in the power of His might."

> *"But we have this treasure in earthen vessels, that the excellency of the power may be of God, and not of us."*
>
> **2 Corinthians 4:7**

4. What does Paul mean when he says, "*I will glory in my infirmities. For when I am weak, then am I strong.*" **(vs. 9-10)**

A. <u>Infirmities</u> – i.e., in my human weakness; my human inability.

B. Meaning weak in the sense that as long as you're in your physical body, in the flesh, you're weak, i.e., you have limitations.

C. It is then that God's power, is within you, i.e., the anointing is within you. It is then that God is glorified through you because when you die and leave your body, then you don't need the anointing because you'll be with Him.

## IV. JESUS IS OUR EXAMPLE NOT PAUL

**Note**: No where in the Bible does it say to use Paul as our example. It says Jesus left us an example to follow.

1. Jesus was never sick. Try and find the page in the Bible that says He was - it's not in there. The only reference would be the time when he hung on a cross and became your substitute.

2. If Paul was sick and never got healed, that's no reason for us to be sick. He didn't die for you or me. If God said to Paul to keep it, that would make God responsible for the sickness and that he was approving it. Acts 10:38, clearly shows us that sickness is from satan not from God.

3. If God wouldn't heal Paul then God is a respecter of persons - healing one, and refusing the other.

> *"Confess your faults one to another, and pray one for another, that ye may be healed. The effectual fervent prayer of a righteous man availeth much."*
>
> **James 5:16**
>
> *"Then Peter opened his mouth, and said, Of a truth I perceive that God is no respecter of persons."*
>
> **Acts 10:34**

4. If God is asking Paul to bear our sicknesses, then Jesus didn't bear them all.

> *"That it might be fulfilled which was spoken by Esaias the prophet, saying, Himself took our infirmities, and bare our sicknesses."*
>
> **Matthew 8:17**

## V. PAUL WAS NOT SICK

1. In **1 Corinthians 11:23-30**, Paul talks about the Lord's Supper. In this discourse he points out that one of the reasons why some believers are sick and even die early is

because they do not discern the Lord's body. If Paul was sick then this would have been a good place for the church at Corinth to write back to Paul and say, "*Well how come you're sick? Did you not discern the Lord's body*?" Wouldn't they have been able to challenge Paul with the same thing?

> *"For he that eateth and drinketh unworthily, eateth and drinketh damnation to himself, not discerning the Lord's body. For this cause many are weak and sickly among you, and many sleep."*
>
> **1 Corinthians 11:29,30**

2. In **2 Corinthians 12:10** - Paul lists the various challenges that he had endured as a believer. Notice the word sickness isn't mentioned at all. If Paul was sick as much as people say he was, it seems like Paul should have mentioned something.

> *"Therefore I take pleasure in infirmities, in reproaches, in necessities, in persecutions, in distresses for Christ's sake: for when I am weak, then am I strong."*
>
> **2 Corinthians 12:10**

3. In **2 Corinthians 6:3-10** – Paul once again catalogues the different types of hardships that he had faced and not once did he mention the word sickness or disease.

> *"We put no stumbling block in anyones path, so that our ministry will not be discredited. Rather, as servants of God we commend ourselves in every way: in great endurance; in troubles, hardships and distresses; in beatings, imprisonments and riots; in hard work, sleepless nights and hunger; in purity, understanding, patience and kindness; in the Holy Spirit and in sincere love; in truthful speech and in the power of God; with weapons of righteousness in the right hand and in the left; through glory and dishonor, bad report and good report; genuine, yet regarded as impostors; known, yet regarded as unknown; dying, and yet we live on; beaten, and yet not killed; sorrowful, yet always rejoicing; poor, yet making many rich; having nothing, and yet possessing everything."*
>
> **2 Corinthians 6:3-10 (NIV)**

4. In **2 Corinthians 11:23-27** - Again there is no sickness mentioned here either.

> *"Are they servants of Christ? (I am out of my mind to talk like this.) I am more. I have worked much harder, been in prison more frequently, been flogged more severely, and been exposed to death again and again. Five times I received from the Jews the forty lashes minus one. Three times I was*

> *beaten with rods, once I was stoned, three times I was shipwrecked, I spent a night and a day in the open sea, I have been constantly on the move. I have been in danger from rivers, in danger from bandits, in danger from my own countrymen, in danger from Gentiles; in danger in the city, in danger in the country, in danger at sea; and in danger from false brothers. I have labored and toiled and have often gone without sleep; I have known hunger and thirst and have often gone without food; I have been cold and naked."*
>
> **2 Corinthians 11:23-27 (NIV)**

5. In **Acts 14:3-10** – Paul and Barnabas preached the gospel and the Lord confirmed his word with sings and wonders. But ask yourself this question: How could a man who is standing up before an audience sick, unable to get well, preach deliverance and healing to them and encourage faith in them to get healed when he couldn't get himself healed? The question will run through your mind, "*How come you're not healed? What is there to make me believe that it will work for me if it won't work for you?*"

> *"So Paul and Barnabas spent considerable time there, speaking boldly for the Lord, who confirmed the message of his grace by enabling them to do miraculous signs and wonders."*
>
> **Acts 14:3 (NIV)**

> **Note**: The reason why people like to use Paul as their excuse for being sick is because he was the foremost leader of the Word of God. He wrote two-thirds of the New Testament himself. The bottom line is that we are not to look at circumstances and experiences of others to determine what God's will is. We must remember that divine healing is not a fact because people get healed, but is a fact because Jesus took your infirmities and bore your sicknesses. Salvation isn't dependent on people getting saved. Salvation is dependent on the work of Calvary.

6. In **Acts 19:11-12** - God did extraordinary miracles through Paul. If Paul was sick and couldn't get healed, what in the world would inspire these people (that the aprons were laid on) that they could get healed?

7. One tradition is that Paul had an eye disease because of what he wrote to the churches in Galatia. Keep in mind that most of his letters were written from prison and dictated to a secretary, but in this instance, He wrote this himself.

> *"Ye know how through infirmity of the flesh I preached the gospel unto you at the first. And my temptation which was in my flesh ye despised not, nor rejected; but received me as an angel of God, even as Christ Jesus. Where*

> *is then the blessedness ye spake of? For I bear you record, that, if it had been possible, ye would have plucked out your own eyes, and have given them to me."*
>
> **Galatians 4:13-15**

8. We are to be fit for the Master's use. How are you going to do good works and be effective for God, when you're sick or laid up at the hospital in traction? That hinders you from working doesn't it? You can't work effectively when you're sick. Think of all the sick people you know who can't do any good works because they're bound to that hospital bed or wheelchair. And not only are they bound but everyone else in the house is also hindered from doing good works because they have to wait on that person hand and foot.

> *"If a man therefore purge himself from these, he shall be a vessel unto honour, sanctified, and meet for the master's use, and prepared unto every good work."*
>
> **2 Timothy 2:21**
>
> *"That the man of God may be perfect, thoroughly furnished unto all good works."*
>
> **2 Timothy 3:17**
>
> *"Who gave himself for us, that he might redeem us from all iniquity, and purify unto himself a peculiar people, zealous of good works."*
>
> **Titus 2:14**
>
> *"This is a faithful saying, and these things I will that thou affirm constantly, that they which have believed in God might be careful to maintain good works. These things are good and profitable unto men."*
>
> **Titus 3:8**

> **Note**: If Paul was sick and God told him to remain sick, then it would be the first time from Genesis to Revelation that God told anybody to stay sick. And that by virtue of itself would invalidate the Bible because the Bible says that God is no respecter of persons. If God healed everybody else and not Paul, then He would be a respecter of persons. There are some bible translations, which say that Paul was sick or had physical ailments. And it is these various translations which people use as an excuse to argue the face that everybody doesn't get healed. If anyone actually believed that it was God's will for them to be sick and that God was getting glory out of it, or that God was teaching them something,

or even chastening them with sickness or disease because they've been bad children, if that were true, that would mean that every aspirin or medication you took would be in direct conflict to the perfect will of God for you to be sick. Every time you went to the doctor you would be in rebellion to the will of God. I thank God for doctors. I've heard folks make statements that these are the healing agents which the Lord has given us today. If that's so, didn't God know that doctors were going to work against God's will by trying to get you healed if it's God's will for you to be sick. If it's true that sickness and disease is God's will, then you should never seek any help for it but accept it with joy, because the minute you seek help, you would be in direct conflict with God's will. If God made you sick for his glory and you are trying to get well, that's resistance isn't it? Not only that, but if you really wanted to be in the center of God's perfect will, then you should pray that God would afflict you with sickness or multiply what you already have. The bottom line is that satan has sold the church a bill of goods about Paul just to keep the church in bondage.

**EX**: "When my aunt died of cancer, all 4 of her children got saved." Would that be God's best? Does your aunt need to die in order for her children to be saved? Why should we settle for one mother dying and getting 4 people saved as a result of it, when Jesus died 2000 years ago to get the whole world saved. Can God take a bad situation and turn it around for good? Yes, but remember the Lord wasn't the cause for the bad situation to begin with. Romans 8:28 tells us that, "*All things work together for good to them that love God, to them who are the called according to his purpose.*" It doesn't say that all things are good does it? Whatever satan does, God can make some good come out of it. If satan destroys a person's life, God can still work it around so that four people get saved out of it, but that's not God's best so why settle for that.

## VI. CONCLUSION

A. Paul was not sick. His thorn in the flesh was not a physical ailment but a demon that was sent to harass Paul.

B. The only suffering a Christian should go through is persecution.

C. God has provided a way of escape for us through His Word.

**- Selah -**

# LESSON 11

# MINISTERING TO THE SICK

## I. THE ANOINTING ON THE MINISTRY OF JESUS

1. Jesus ministered as the Son of man.

> *"Let this mind be in you, which was also in Christ Jesus: Who, being in the form of God, thought it not robbery to be equal with God: But made himself of no reputation, and took upon him the form of a servant, and was made in the likeness of men: And being found in fashion as a man, he humbled himself, and became obedient unto death, even the death of the cross."*
>
> **Philippians 2:5-8**

2. He was dependent on the anointing of the Holy Spirit.

> *"The Spirit of the Lord is upon me, because he hath anointed me to preach the gospel to the poor; he hath sent me to heal the brokenhearted, to preach deliverance to the captives, and recovering of sight to the blind, to set at liberty them that are bruised, To preach the acceptable year of the Lord."*
>
> **Luke 4:18,19**
>
> *"How God anointed Jesus of Nazareth with the Holy Ghost and with power: who went about doing good, and healing all that were oppressed of the devil; for God was with him."*
>
> **Acts 10:38**

3. He had the anointing without measure.

> *"For he whom God hath sent speaketh the words of God: for God giveth not the Spirit by measure unto him."*
>
> **John 3:34**

4. He walked in the reputation of the Father through the power of the Holy Spirit.

> *"But Jesus answered them, My Father worketh hitherto, and I work."*
>
> **John 5:17**
>
> *"I am come in my Father's name, and ye receive me not: if another shall come in his own name, him ye will receive."*
>
> **John 5:43**
>
> *"Jesus answered them, I told you, and ye believed not: the works that I do in my Father's name, they bear witness of me."*
>
> **John 10:25**
>
> *"Ye men of Israel, hear these words; Jesus of Nazareth, a man approved of God among you by miracles and wonders and signs, which God did by him in the midst of you, as ye yourselves also know."*
>
> **Acts 2:22**

## II. THE HEALING MINISTRY OF JESUS

1. There are 24 specific accounts recorded in the Gospels.

2. Various methods were used such as the spoken Word; the healing touch; clay of spit; fingers in ears, etc.

3. Ten out of the 24 were healed through their faith (42%) and fourteen (58%) were healed through the gifts of healings, working of miracles, etc.

4. On many occasions Jesus initiated the healing.

> *"On another Sabbath he went into the synagogue and was teaching, and a man was there whose right hand was shriveled. The Pharisees and the teachers of the law were looking for a reason to accuse Jesus, so they watched him closely to see if he would heal on the Sabbath. But Jesus knew what they were thinking and said to the man with the shriveled hand, Get up and stand in front of everyone. So he got up and stood there. Then Jesus said to them, I ask you, which is lawful on the Sabbath: to do good or to do evil, to save life or to destroy it? He looked around at them all, and then said to the man, Stretch out your hand. He did so, and his hand was completely restored."*
>
> **Luke 6:6-10 (NIV)**

*"Soon afterward, Jesus went to a town called Nain, and his disciples and a large crowd went along with him. As he approached the town gate, a dead person was being carried out–the only son of his mother, and she was a widow. And a large crowd from the town was with her. When the Lord saw her, his heart went out to her and he said, Don't cry. Then he went up and touched the coffin, and those carrying it stood still. He said, Young man, I say to you, get up! The dead man sat up and began to talk, and Jesus gave him back to his mother. They were all filled with awe and praised God."*

**Luke 7:11-16 (NIV)**

*"On a Sabbath Jesus was teaching in one of the synagogues, and a woman was there who had been crippled by a spirit for eighteen years. She was bent over and could not straighten up at all. When Jesus saw her, he called her forward and said to her, Woman, you are set free from your infirmity. Then he put his hands on her, and immediately she straightened up and praised God."*

**Luke 13:10-13 (NIV)**

*"One Sabbath, when Jesus went to eat in the house of a prominent Pharisee, he was being carefully watched. There in front of him was a man suffering from dropsy. Jesus asked the Pharisees and experts in the law, Is it lawful to heal on the Sabbath or not? But they remained silent. So taking hold of the man, he healed him and sent him away."*

**Luke 14:1-4 (NIV)**

## III. THE MINISTRY OF BELIEVERS

1. We must depend on the anointing of the Holy Spirit. Jesus did and so must we.

*"And it shall come to pass in that day, that his burden shall be taken away from off thy shoulder, and his yoke from off thy neck, and the yoke shall be destroyed because of the anointing."*

**Isaiah 10:27**

*"Not that we are fit (qualified and sufficient in ability) of ourselves to form personal judgments or to claim or count anything as coming from us, but our power and ability and sufficiency are from God."*

**2 Corinthians 3:5 (AMP)**

*"In conclusion, be strong in the Lord [be empowered through your union with Him]; draw your strength from Him [that strength which His boundless*

*might provides].”*

**Ephesians 6:10 (AMP)**

*“I have strength for all things in Christ Who empowers me [I am ready for anything and equal to anything through Him Who infuses inner strength into me; I am self- sufficient in Christ's sufficiency].”*

**Philippians 4:13 (AMP)**

2. The same Spirit that anointed Jesus anoints us. Our body is His temple.

*“But you will receive power when the Holy Spirit comes on you; and you will be my witnesses in Jerusalem, and in all Judea and Samaria, and to the ends of the earth.”*

**Acts 1:8 (NIV)**

3. The anointing is resident within us. Where we go, He goes, and so does His power.

*“And I will ask the Father, and he will give you another Counselor to be with you forever.”*

**John 14:16 (NIV)**

*“But you have an anointing from the Holy One, and all of you know the truth...As for you, the anointing you received from him remains in you.”*

**1 John 2:20, 27 (NIV)**

4. Believers now walk in the reputation of Jesus. We are to go forth in His name.

*“Then Jesus came to them and said, All authority in heaven and on earth has been given to me. Therefore go and make disciples of all nations, baptizing them in the name of the Father and of the Son and of the Holy Spirit, and teaching them to obey everything I have commanded you. And surely I am with you always, to the very end of the age.”*

**Matthew 28:18-20 (NIV)**

*“He said to them, Go into all the world and preach the good news to all creation. Whoever believes and is baptized will be saved, but whoever does not believe will be condemned. And these signs will accompany those who believe: In my name they will drive out demons; they will speak in new tongues; they will pick up snakes with their hands; and when they drink deadly poison, it will not hurt them at all; they will place their hands on sick people, and they will get well.”*

**Mark 16:15-18 (NIV)**

> *"I have given you authority to trample on snakes and scorpions and to overcome all the power of the enemy; nothing will harm you."*
>
> **Luke 10:19 (NIV)**
>
> *"I tell you the truth, anyone who has faith in me will do what I have been doing. He will do even greater things than these, because I am going to the Father. And I will do whatever you ask in my name, so that the Son may bring glory to the Father. You may ask me for anything in my name, and I will do it."*
>
> **John 14:12-14 (NIV)**

5. The anointing can be increased in our lives. There are several factors, which can effect it. Here are a few to consider:

   A. **The word of God** (Bring yourself into a greater knowledge and understanding of God's word.)

> *"For I am not ashamed of the gospel of Christ: for it is the power of God unto salvation to every one that believeth; to the Jew first, and also to the Greek."*
>
> **Romans 1:16**
>
> *"Let the word of Christ dwell in you richly."*
>
> **Colossians 3:16**

   B. **Prayer** (Look what happened to Moses when He came down off the mountaintop after spending considerable time in the presence of God. The more you know Him, the more you'll become like Him. The end result is that others will see Him through you.)

> *"And it came to pass, when Moses came down from mount Sinai with the two tables of testimony in Moses 'hand, when he came down from the mount, that Moses wist not that the skin of his face shone while he talked with him."*
>
> **Exodus 34:29**
>
> *"Pray without ceasing."*
>
> **1 Thessalonians 5:17**

   C. **Association** (Who we associate with can drastically effect the anointing in and on our lives. Consider Elijah and Elisha. The one received a double portion of

the anointing and as a result was twice as effective. But if we don't protect the anointing it can be diminished and eventually lost.)

> *"Do not be yoked together with unbelievers. For what do righteousness and wickedness have in common? Or what fellowship can light have with darkness? What harmony is there between Christ and Belial? What does a believer have in common with an unbeliever? What agreement is there between the temple of God and idols? For we are the temple of the living God. As God has said: I will live with them and walk among them, and I will be their God, and they will be my people. Therefore come out from them and be separate, says the Lord. Touch no unclean thing, and I will receive you. I will be a Father to you, and you will be my sons and daughters, says the Lord Almighty."*
>
> **2 Corinthians 6:14-18 (NIV)**
>
> *"Do not be misled: Bad company corrupts good character."*
>
> **1 Corinthians 15:33 (NIV)**

D. **Faithfulness** (There's something about a faithful servant that pleases the Master. The end result of faithfulness always produces increase and blessing. Anything less is unacceptable. It really comes down to a heart attitude. If I'm committed to the Lord, then I will undoubtedly want to please Him. And one thing that pleases the Lord is faithfulness. Learn to be faithful to His word and to His Spirit. Remember that faithfulness begins with the little things.)

> *"His lord said unto him, Well done, thou good and faithful servant: thou hast been faithful over a few things, I will make thee ruler over many things: enter thou into the joy of thy lord."*
>
> **Matthew 25:21**
>
> *"If they obey and serve him, they shall spend their days in prosperity, and their years in pleasures."*
>
> **Job 36:11**
>
> *"Moreover it is required in stewards, that a man be found faithful."*
>
> **1 Corinthians 4:2**
>
> *"A faithful man shall abound with blessings."*
>
> **Proverbs 28:20**

## IV. VARIOUS METHODS OF MINISTERING TO THE SICK

1. Anointing oil

> *"Is any sick among you? let him call for the elders of the church; and let them pray over him, anointing him with oil in the name of the Lord: And the prayer of faith shall save the sick, and the Lord shall raise him up; and if he have committed sins, they shall be forgiven him. Confess your faults one to another, and pray one for another, that ye may be healed. The effectual fervent prayer of a righteous man availeth much."*
>
> **James 5:14-16**
>
> *"And they cast out many devils, and anointed with oil many that were sick, and healed them."*
>
> **Mark 6:13**

2. Laying on of hands

> *"And these signs shall follow them that believe; In my name shall they cast out devils; they shall speak with new tongues; They shall take up serpents; and if they drink any deadly thing, it shall not hurt them; they shall lay hands on the sick, and they shall recover."*
>
> **Mark 16:17-18**
>
> *"Therefore leaving the principles of the doctrine of Christ, let us go on unto perfection; not laying again the foundation of repentance from dead works, and of faith toward God, Of the doctrine of baptisms, and of laying on of hands, and of resurrection of the dead, and of eternal judgment."*
>
> **Hebrews 6:1-2**
>
> *"And when Jesus was passed over again by ship unto the other side, much people gathered unto him: and he was nigh unto the sea. And, behold, there cometh one of the rulers of the synagogue, Jairus by name; and when he saw him, he fell at his feet, And besought him greatly, saying, My little daughter lieth at the point of death: I pray thee, come and lay thy hands on her, that she may be healed; and she shall live."*
>
> **Mark 5:21-23**

3. Spoken Word

*"He sent his word, and healed them, and delivered them from their destructions."*

**Psalm 107:20**

*"The centurion answered and said, Lord, I am not worthy that thou shouldest come under my roof: but speak the word only, and my servant shall be healed."*

**Matthew 8:3**

*"For as the rain cometh down, and the snow from heaven, and returneth not thither, but watereth the earth, and maketh it bring forth and bud, that it may give seed to the sower, and bread to the eater: So shall my word be that goeth forth out of my mouth: it shall not return unto me void, but it shall accomplish that which I please, and it shall prosper in the thing whereto I sent it."*

**Isaiah 55:10-11**

*"For verily I say unto you, That whosoever shall say unto this mountain, Be thou removed, and be thou cast into the sea; and shall not doubt in his heart, but shall believe that those things which he saith shall come to pass; he shall have whatsoever he saith."*

**Mark 11:23**

4. Handkerchief or aprons

*"And this continued by the space of two years; so that all they which dwelt in Asia heard the word of the Lord Jesus, both Jews and Greeks. And God wrought special miracles by the hands of Paul: So that from his body were brought unto the sick handkerchiefs or aprons, and the diseases departed from them, and the evil spirits went out of them."*

**Acts 19:10-12**

5. Special manifestations or gifts of the Holy Spirit

*"But all these worketh that one and the selfsame Spirit, dividing to every man severally as he will."*

**1 Corinthians 12:11**

6. Individual's faith alone

> *"Jesus said unto him, If thou canst believe, all things are possible to him that believeth."*
>
> **Mark 9:23**
>
> *"Therefore I say unto you, What things soever ye desire, when ye pray, believe that ye receive them, and ye shall have them."*
>
> **Mark 11:24**

7. Lord's Supper

> *"For I have received of the Lord that which also I delivered unto you, That the Lord Jesus the same night in which he was betrayed took bread: And when he had given thanks, he brake it, and said, Take, eat: this is my body, which is broken for you: this do in remembrance of me. After the same manner also he took the cup, when he had supped, saying, This cup is the new testament in my blood: this do ye, as oft as ye drink it, in remembrance of me. For as often as ye eat this bread, and drink this cup, ye do shew the Lord's death till he come. Wherefore whosoever shall eat this bread, and drink this cup of the Lord, unworthily, shall be guilty of the body and blood of the Lord. But let a man examine himself, and so let him eat of that bread, and drink of that cup. For he that eateth and drinketh unworthily, eateth and drinketh damnation to himself, not discerning the Lord's body. For this cause many are weak and sickly among you, and many sleep. For if we would judge ourselves, we should not be judged."*
>
> **1 Corinthians 11:23-31**

8 Prayer of agreement

> *"Again I say unto you, that if two of you shall agree on earth as touching any thing that they shall ask, it shall be done for them of my Father which is in heaven. For where two or three are gathered together in my name, there am I in the midst of them."*
>
> **Matthew 18:19-20**
>
> *"How should one chase a thousand, and two put ten thousand to flight, except their Rock had sold them, and the LORD had shut them up?"*
>
> **Deuteronomy 32:30**

## V. CONCLUSION

1. If Jesus demonstrated the power of the Holy Spirit in His humanity, realize the potential of your ministry under the power of the same Spirit.

2. The greatest results are shown in the healing ministry after the preaching of the Word, which releases faith in the hearts of the listeners.

> *"So then faith cometh by hearing, and hearing by the word of God."*
> **Romans 10:17**

3. To the degree you separate yourself to God, determines the degree that God will manifest Himself in your life and ministry.

4. Which method should I use when praying for the sick? Whichever one seems appropriate at the time. Usually you will have several to choose from. Go with the one that seems good in your heart.

**- Selah -**

# LESSON 12

# THE HEALING MINISTRY OF JESUS

| CASE IN CHRONOLOGICAL ORDER | AREA | REFERENCES | HEALING CATEGORY | METHOD USED |
|---|---|---|---|---|
| | | | | |
| 1. Man with leprosy | Galilee | Matthew 8:1-4<br>Mark 1:40-45<br>Luke 5:12-15 | Gift of healing | Spoken word<br>Healing touch |
| 2. Centurion's servant | Capernaum | Matthew 8:5-13<br>Luke 7:1-10 | Own faith | Spoken word<br>In proxy |
| 3. Peter's mother in law | Capernaum | Matthew 8:14-15<br>Mark 1:29-31<br>Luke 4:38-39 | Gift of healing | Spoken word<br>Healing touch |
| 4. Man with palsy | Capernaum | Matthew 9:1-8<br>Mark 2:1-12<br>Luke 5:17-26 | Own faith | Spoken word |
| 5. Jairus daughter | Capernaum | Matthew 9:18-26<br>Mark 5:22-43<br>Luke 8:40-56 | Own faith<br>Gift of healing<br>Gift of special faith<br>Working of miracles | Spoken word<br>Healing touch |
| 6. Women with the issue of blood | Capernaum | Matthew 9:20-22<br>Mark 5:25-34<br>Luke 8:43-48 | Own faith | Contact |
| 7. Two blind men | Galilee | Matthew 9:27-31 | Own faith | Spoken word<br>Healing Touch |
| 8. Dumb man | Galilee | Matthew 9:32,33 | Cast out demon | Spoken word |
| 9. Man with withered hand | Galilee or Jerusalem | Matthew 12:9-13<br>Mark 3:1-5<br>Luke 6:6 10 | Gift of healing | Spoken word |
| | | | | |

| CASE IN CHRONOLOGICAL ORDER | AREA | REFERENCES | HEALING CATEGORY | METHOD USED |
|---|---|---|---|---|
| | | | | |
| 10. Blind and dumb demoniac | Galilee | Matthew 12:22<br>Luke 11:14 | Cast out demon | Spoken word |
| 11. Canaanite woman's daughter | Canaan | Matthew 15:21-28<br>Mark 7:24-30 | Own faith | Spoken word<br>In proxy |
| 12. Boy with deaf and dumb spirit | Caesarea | Matthew 17:14-19<br>Mark 9:17-29<br>Luke 9:38-43 | Own faith<br>Cast out demon | Spoken word |
| 13. Two blind men including Bartimaeus | Jericho | Matthew 20:29-34<br>Mark 10:46-52<br>Luke 18:35-43 | Own faith | Spoken word<br>Healing touch |
| 14. Deaf and speech impediment | Decapolis | Mark 7:31-35 | Gift of healing | Spoken word<br>Fingers in ears;<br>Spit & touched tongue |
| 15. Blind man | Bethsaida | Mark 8:22-26 | Gift of healing | Spit on eyes<br>Laid hands twice |
| 16. Widow's son | Nain in Galilee | Luke 7:11-16 | Gift of healing<br>Gift of special faith<br>Working of miracles | Spoken word |
| 17. Woman with spirit of infirmity | Perea | Luke 13:10-17 | Gift of healing | Spoken word<br>Healing touch |
| 18. Man with dropsy | Perea | Luke 14:1-4 | Gift of healing | Healing touch |
| 19. Ten lepers | Samaria and Galilee | Luke 17:11-19 | Own faith | Spoken word |
| 20. Malchus' ear | Jerusalem | Luke 22:47-51 | Working of miracles | Healing touch |
| 21. Nobleman's' son | Cana | John 4:46-54 | Own faith | Spoken word |
| 22. Impotent man at pool of Bethesda | Jerusalem | John 5:1-15 | Gift of healing | Spoken word |
| 23. Man born blind | Jerusalem | John 9:1-7 | Gift of healing | Clay of spit<br>Touched eyes |
| 24. Lazarus | Bethany | John 11:1-46 | Gift of healing<br>Gift of special faith<br>Working of miracles | Spoken word |
| | | | | |

**To order books and CD'S by Rev. Todd Levin or to contact him for speaking engagements, please write to:**

**Todd Levin Ministries International**
**P.O. Box 826**
**Bell Vernon, Pa 15012**

*Email us*
**toddlevinministries@hotmail.com**

*Website*:
**www.toddlevinministries.com**

Made in the USA
San Bernardino, CA
17 March 2016